Follow The Hearts

By the same author

Hearts and Hibs – Capital Classics, 1998

Follow The Hearts

Following the fortunes
of Heart of Midlothian FC
for over thirty five years

by

Mike Smith

Follow The Hearts
Following the fortunes
of Heart of Midlothian FC
for over thirty five years

© Mike Smith 2004

First published in Great Britain 2004
by WritersPrintshop

ISBN 1904623077

Designed by
Rob Oldfield

Acknowledgements

Thanks to
the SNS Agency in Glasgow
for the use of photographs in this book;
to Lawrence Broadie and Lewis Broadie
who put so much work into jambos.net
and ATB respectively
– the best places to read about Hearts –
and who encourage and occasionally harass
(only kidding lads!)
me to write articles, subsequently,
giving me the idea for writing this book.

To Gavin Aitchison who kindly offered
to help with photographs.

To my wife Pat to whom I confess
I wasn't really at a personnel conference in
Ballahuish in November 2003
I was in Bordeaux watching Hearts most
famous win in Europe.

Grateful thanks, also, to Chas Jones
of WritersPrintshop for his help
with this publication.

And to Heart of Midlothian Football club,
without which, life just wouldn't be the same.

This book is dedicated to my late father who gave
me the encouragement to
write in the first place.

Mike Smith
January 2004

Contents

INTRODUCTION

I know what you're thinking. Another book about Hearts with little to say. And if you're not a Hearts supporter, well there are worse things to spend your money on. If you're a Hibby, you may not be able to read this anyway so I can say what I like. Anyway, there aren't many pictures in this book so put it back on the shelf, there's a good lad.

I had thought about calling this book 'This is My Story'. But then I thought who the hell would want to read the story of an overweight, balding bespectacled man who spends every other Saturday going to Tynecastle to 'get right behind the team'. Then again more than thirty five years of the ritual that is following the fortunes of Heart of Midlothian Football Club will not make the most riveting of reads either, particularly if those who aren't of a maroon persuasion have parted with hard earned cash for it. But for those whose life revolves -and has evolved -around following Hearts then I hope they can relate to parts of this book. The joy, the pain, the anguish - life is never dull being a Hearts fan.

My wife couldn't understand why I left her, on the day our first child was due to be born, to go to the Scottish Cup Final in 1986, We lived in Aberdeen at the time. Granted, I took her point it was 140 miles from our home to Hampden and she wanted me to be in the Granite City for the birth. And seven days earlier she had been in severe pain whilst I was watching Hearts throw the league championship away at Dens Park. But I pointed out that while she could have more babies (and she did)

Hearts might never get to another Scottish Cup Final (they did). I put her resultant wailing and threats of divorce down to the hormones - well, it can affect people in different ways. My own wailing came after a 3-0 defeat for the Jambos at the hands of Aberdeen. As it was my wife gave birth to a bouncing baby girl, a week after the cup final. Three consecutive Saturdays in May 1986 when I was an emotional wreck.

Okay, I may not have been the perfect father. Okay, I did miss my youngest daughter's fourth birthday as a result of being in Madrid to see Hearts being hammered by Atletico. I may have left the family holiday in Lossiemouth to travel down to the midweek Aberdeen v. Hearts League Cup tie. And my older daughter's twelfth birthday was spent in the thronging streets of Edinburgh watching Hearts parade the Scottish Cup in 1998. Fair points, I concede.

But I know there are thousands of other people for whom Follow The Hearts is more than a way of life - it is life. This book is for them.

Mike Smith
April 2004

1

Life Begins at Brockville
1968-1972

1970's stalwart George Fleming
in action against Dumbarton at
Tynecastle

1968-1972

OCTOBER 1968. Friday evening in a house in Cumbernauld, an overspill of 1960s Glasgow. My father came home from work and lapsed into Parliamo Glasgow. 'Awright, son, ah've gorra perra tickets furra game ramorra'. He wanted to take his six year old son to a football match but was determined I wasn't going to be embroiled in the religious bigotry that can afflict Celtic and Rangers. So for my first match he took me to Brockville Park to see Falkirk v. Hearts. A good job Esther Rantzen hadn't thought of Childline at that time. My dear father's intention, however well meant, was to bring me up as a Falkirk 'Bairn' (for the uninitiated, Falkirk's nickname is The Bairns). The experience left its mark on me. Brockville was a sea of maroon and white that day and the buoyant Hearts support was in excellent voice. As this was my first game, the bug that is being a Jambo bit me. Despite my father's best efforts, I had no interest in Falkirk. In fact I took a good deal of convincing that Falkirk were the home team, out -numbered as they were by two to one by those from Edinburgh. As befitting an instant love affair, Hearts won 3-1 that day and, for me, life would never be the same again.

I had vaguely remembered something about Hearts being in the Scottish Cup final six months earlier but in the 1960s and for most of the 1970s, the Cup final wasn't live on television and, indeed, close to a full league programme was played on the same day. This was a shade before my time as a Jambo but I know people who, to this day, speak of their crushing disappointment as they trudged out of Hampden Park on a dreary April day in 1968. Hearts had typically raised expectations by knocking out Rangers on the way to the final (44,000 fans packed into Tynecastle on a Wednesday night witnessed Donald Ford score a late winner in the replay) although equally typically, Hearts struggled against Morton in the semi-final, requiring another replay. The Jambos were favourites to lift the famous old trophy for the first time since their famous victory over Celtic twelve years earlier. I wasn't at Hampden but by all accounts it was a tepid display from the boys in maroon and Dunfermline Athletic (yes, Dunfermline Athletic) won rather more easily than the 3-1 score suggests. Having lost the league championship on the last day of the season three years earlier, it was another severe blow for those in maroon. But despair is a constant companion of the Hearts supporter and it wouldn't be long before it would become like a soul brother to me.

The 1960s marked Hearts descent from the top of Scottish football. The 'Terrible Trio' forward line of Conn, Bauld and Wardhaugh had dominated the game in the late 1950s and the Hearts team that ran away with the 1958 League championship will probably never have their achievement eclipsed. They lost just one game, won the league by thirteen points and scored an incredible 132 goals in just thirty-four games. An average of very nearly four goals a game. I envy those Hearts supporters who lived through that era. While Hearts may lift another trophy before I leave this earth it will never be done again in such devastating fashion.

By the time I had been introduced to the boys in maroon they were on a downward spiral that would eventually end in relegation, massive debts and the club nearly folding altogether. Now I'm not paranoid but, honest guv', that had nothing to do with me.

In 1968 Hearts were managed by Johnny Harvey who had been assistant to the legendary Tommy Walker at a time when Hearts ruled the country. When Walker left Tynecastle in 1966, Harvey took over as manager, rumoured at the time to be a move he never really wanted. One of the many heartfelt gripes of the average Hearts supporter is the frequent sale of players who happen to show more than your average ability. The first player I can recall whose departure from Tynecastle caused a stir was Arthur Mann, a cultured left back who left for Manchester City in 1968 and helped the Maine Road club lift the English League Championship the following year. Being only six years old, I didn't understand the complexities of the transfer system but I remember my father remarking that Hearts had seemingly accepted the first offer made and Mann was on his way for a ridiculously low transfer fee. Hard to believe, I know, but that may have happened once or twice since...

The 1970s was to be the decade where Hearts slide to near oblivion gathered pace with alarming ferocity. Johnny Harvey perhaps saw what was coming and bailed out and Hearts next manager in 1970 was, unusually for the club at that time, a man who had no previous connection with Tynecastle – Bobby Seith. Seith had been part of the Dundee team that won the Scottish

League Championship in 1962 and had gone close to success in the European Cup the following season. His coaching credentials were not in doubt but there was uneasiness in Gorgie apparent even to an eight year old. A decade had passed since the glory days and few could see them returning under the new manager.

It didn't help that Celtic were dominating Scottish football like no other team before or since. The legendary Jock Stein had built a team that had won the European Cup in 1967 and, three years later, had reached another European Cup Final (although unfancied Feyenoord didn't follow the script in 1970). Consequently there was next to no chance of Hearts winning the league championship as they had done to mark the beginning of the 1960s so our only hope of success lay in the cups.

My first painful disappointment as a Hearts fan – and many more would blight my life with disturbing regularity – came a few months after Seith's appointment. Hearts had been drawn at home against Hibs in the fourth round of the Scottish Cup in 1971 and the tie was the one everyone wanted to see. With Tynecastle packed, Hibs took an early lead when John Hazel was left with the freedom of Gorgie to head home a free-kick. Hearts fought back with a second half equaliser from Kevin Hegarty but just as it looked like a replay at Easter Road, Arthur Duncan fired in a shot that almost burst the net to give Hibs victory. Losing a cup-tie is bad enough but at home….and to the Hibees! The pain was felt acutely for days afterwards. 'Never mind, son' my father offered, 'you'll get used to it' said with a smugness and a 'Well, you chose to follow Hearts' tone. Thanks Dad.

Hearts had toyed with the unthinkable idea of

relegation that season but the first half of the 1970s was a story of midtable mediocrity. Hearts were awful but thanks to a ridiculously large eighteen-team league were able to finish above the likes of Arbroath, East Fife and Dumbarton fairly regularly. But it wasn't pretty to watch. Attendances began to drop alarmingly at Tynecastle and apathy began to reign. Nowhere near good enough to challenge Celtic but doing enough to avoid the ultimate ignominy of relegation to the backwaters of Scottish football, Hearts decline since the heady days of the 1950s was rapid – and it had still to peak.

It's not unknown for one half of Edinburgh to be struggling while the other half enjoys a modicum of success. Whilst Hearts were slip, sliding away, former Famous Five legend Eddie Turnbull had built a Hibs side that was not only challenging the Old Firm but also competing in European competition. Such idealism was just a pipedream for Hearts fans who had to make do with seeing their team compete in the country's first sponsored competition – The Texaco Cup. In retrospect, this was akin to getting a cheap plastic key ring at a funfair instead of the goldfish – clubs in the Texaco Cup weren't good enough to qualify for the U.E.F.A. Cup – but Hearts supporters at the time lapped it up. Particularly when Hearts reached the final in 1971. The Texaco Cup was open to English and Irish clubs as well as Scots and some decent English sides such as Burnley and Oldham Athletic would come to Tynecastle for midweek games that attracted fairly sizeable attendances. Hearts won an epic semi-final tie against Motherwell in 1971 and so faced Wolverhampton Wanderers in the two-legged final. The first leg was at Tynecastle and attracted a crowd of over 25,000 such was the interest in the competition.

Wolves were a top side at that time with the likes of Irish internationalist Derek Dougan and Scots cap Hugh Curran in their team and they duly showed their class by winning the first leg 3-1. That appeared to end the contest but, typically, Hearts won the second leg at Molineux but lost 3-2 on aggregate. It had been a rare moment of excitement in an otherwise drab season.

The Hearts team of 1971 wasn't the most talented in the club's history but they did have one of the most skilful forwards in Scottish football in Donald Ford. Fordie was a hero to Hearts fans eager to cling on to the hope that their team was still among the country's best and he was to be part of Scotland's World Cup squad of 1974 in West Germany. Ford was a shining light in a somewhat dull Hearts team which struggled to make any progress, particularly in the League Cup which at that time was played in a sectional format in the first round. Section winners progressed to a knock-out stage. However Hearts fans didn't have much of an inkling of what that was all about as their team failed to qualify from the sectional stage for a remarkable twelve years from 1962 to 1974. The nadir of this was 1972 when Hearts failed to progress from a group which consisted of Airdrieonians, Berwick Rangers and Dumbarton. Reflect on that the next time you head for The Diggers after a heavy defeat from either of the Old Firm.

By 1972 I was beginning to wonder if Hearts would ever get close to winning anything again. There was brief hope in the spring of that year when Hearts reached the quarter final of the Scottish Cup. There were collective groans around Gorgie when Hearts were drawn away to Celtic but, against all odds as someone once sang, Hearts drew 1-1 at Celtic Park to force Jock Stein's men to a replay in Gorgie. When you look at Tynecastle today it looks a packed house when there are 17,000 fans there. On March 27th 1972, more than 40,000 packed into the old Tynecastle terracing for the replay – the last 40,000 plus crowd to turn up in Gorgie. The feeling was that if Hearts could beat Celtic they could beat anyone and they would be among the favourites to win the trophy. But Celtic sneaked a somewhat fortuitous 1-0 win and so Hearts Scottish Cup dreams were over for another year. Older Hearts fans were already bemoaning the fact that it had been sixteen years since the last Scottish Cup victory – they would have been apoplectic if someone had told them it would be more than a quarter of a century still until maroon and white ribbons would adorn the old trophy once more.

Anguish in Gorgie increased considerably when a half decent Hibs team upset the odds and defeated Rangers in the semi-final but we breathed again when Celtic put the Hibees in their place by thrashing them 6-1 in the final. Hibs in the Scottish Cup final was like the 6-1 scoreline – it doesn't happen very often!

Towards the end of season 1971-72 there was one game that lightened the gloom in Gorgie. Hearts thrashed Celtic 4-1 at Tynecastle in April and while Jock Stein's men had already wrapped up a seventh successive league championship by then, hammering the best team in Scotland – and, at that time, one of the best in Europe – was sweet indeed. Almost as sweet as beating the Hibees (but not quite).

Season 1972-73 was a season that Hearts fans would rather forget. I was ten years old, going on eleven and for the first time seriously began to doubt my decision in following Edinburgh's finest. The tell-tale signs that

9

Hearts were slipping ever deeper into the quagmire were shown in the League Cup when Bobby Seith's men finished third in their section. A section containing four teams. And New Years Day 1973 saw a team from across Edinburgh score, erm, seven goals without reply at Tynecastle. Hibs fans – some of who weren't even born then – still taunt us about that game to this day but, as the dominant team in Edinburgh, Hearts are there to be shot at by the wee team. Anyway, Hearts finished in tenth position in the First Division at the end of that miserable season, with a win at Ibrox in December easily the highlight. But Hearts struggled badly to score goals – that lot from Easter Road had scored nearly twice as many as Hearts in the league – and with the Centenary season approaching, Jambos were screaming for action to be taken. Fans complained that Hearts were too negative, too defensive – I just thought we were rubbish. How could Hearts have fallen from potential league champions to a team of duds in just seven years? A question many Hearts fans were asking.

Changes had to be made for season 1973-74. They were. And for a few glorious weeks at the start of the centenary season it looked like the glory days were back.

2

The Century's Up
1973-1976

A 'well done' for striker Willie Gibson
from manager John Hagart

1973-1976

SCARCELY A WEEK went by in the summer of 1973 that Hearts weren't linked to one player or another. While I was bopping around to the cultured sound of 1970s glam rock stars Slade, much was made in the Scottish press of how Hearts were preparing for a big splash in the transfer market in an attempt to get success in the centenary year of 1974. There was little doubt the side needed a major overhaul if it was to get anywhere near the Old Firm, particularly Celtic whose domination of the League Championship was becoming monotonous. To quote a line from one of Slade's most famous numbers, I was 'Far, Far, Away with my head up in the clouds'. The mental scars of the New Years Day annihilation would take some time to heal and even I, as an eleven year old in Aberdeen, felt strongly that the Hearts board of directors needed to do something to show they cared about a club whose centenary season was about to celebrated by more than just people in Edinburgh. And, to be fair to the guys in the suits, they did.

As season 1973-74 approached manager Bobby Seith made some major moves in the transfer market as the importance of the season ahead was recognised. Following the arrival of winger Kenny Aird from St. Johnstone and John Stevenson from Coventry City, Seith made an audacious attempt to sign the Airdrieonians duo of Drew Busby and Drew Jarvie who, despite the Lanarkshire club struggling in the league, were proving a potent forward partnership. In the end Seith managed to sign just one of the Drews – Busby, the one with the hair – while Jarvie headed north for an illustrious career with Aberdeen. Another new arrival at Tynecastle was winger Bobby Prentice from Celtic and it was a revamped Hearts side that began the 1973-74 season hoping to bring silverware to Gorgie for the first time in more than a decade.

For me, 1973 was a time of awakening. Not that I had been asleep since 1962 you understand but by now my parents had divorced and I was now living in Aberdeen where my mother's family came from. Now, sampling the delights of the Granite City – there are some I'm told – naturally meant a vast restriction in the number of Hearts games I could go to. My trips to Tynecastle were no longer a regular feature although I doubt if any Hearts fan has seen their team at Pittodrie Stadium more times than I in the past thirty years. Back in 1973 if you couldn't get to the game you had to rely on crackly BBC Radio's 'Sport on Two' on a Saturday afternoon or an even more crackly Radio Scotland's Sportsreel which only went on air ten minutes before half-time meaning you spent much of the opening half hour wondering how many goals Hearts were behind (Most Hearts fans, particularly those who can recall the 1960s and 70s have an almost natural pessimism and, if you know your history if you'll pardon the phrase, you'll understand why)

There was hope, however, as the ponderous League Cup got underway in August 1973. There's always hope for every team in August (except if you're a Hibby leaving

Tynecastle after a 5-1 drubbing.....) Hearts new look team defeated Partick Thistle 2-0 at Tynecastle in the opening game but the new found optimism soon drifted away as Hearts fell behind Dundee and St. Johnstone and so failed to make it yet again to the knock-out stages of the competition. Not since Hearts lifted the trophy in 1962 had they qualified from the group stages – it was now becoming something of a running joke with other clubs almost praying they'd be drawn in the same section as the maroons.

Early season optimism was beginning to evaporate quicker that the steam from a Tynecastle pie although those who like to believe that other forces are at work – and I'm not inferring anything against Lothian & Borders finest here you understand – were prepared to read something into the fact that Hearts opened the league championship campaign with a 3-2 victory over Morton at Cappielow Park. Nothing too exceptional about that you may argue but Hearts won with a hat-trick of penalty kicks – Donald Ford writing himself into the history books as the first Hearts player to manage such a feat. If Hearts were looking to create history in their centenary season then they had certainly started in the correct fashion. For those of us still shell-shocked after the seven goal hammering on New Years Day, this was a bit of a tonic before the next league fixture – the return of Hibernian to Tynecastle with gloating Hibees having inflicted nine months of misery on those of us who support the big team in Edinburgh. Even though I was 130 miles away, I still felt the pain, something my mother couldn't begin to understand.

It was an illustration of the changes made at Tynecastle that only four of the Hearts team that began the New Year mauling started the rematch nine months later. Youngsters Sneddon and Cant as well as newcomers Busby, Stevenson and Prentice were all sampling their first taste of an Edinburgh derby and their youthful innocence was a major factor in how the game would unfurl. Hibs had former Airdrieonians goalkeeper Roddy McKenzie making his capital derby debut but it was to prove an unhappy occasion for Drew Busby's former team-mate.

A crowd of 30,000 created a frantic atmosphere and the game kicked off with Hearts looking the more confident side. Busby and Ford were already looking to have forged a meaningful partnership and there was plenty of width with both Aird and Prentice foraging down the flanks. Hibs seemed to be struggling to contain this new look Hearts side and keeper McKenzie looked less than comfortable in his new environment. And it was from a mistake from the Hibs number one that Hearts went ahead after twenty minutes. Youngster Jim Jefferies, showing the maturity of a senior professional, floated a cross into the Hibs penalty box, which didn't appear to pose any threat. McKenzie decided to come out and collect but – to the horror of his fellow defenders – completely misjudged the flight of the ball. In the ensuing confusion in the penalty box, Hibs full-back Erich Schaedler headed into his own net after a desperate attempt to clear the danger. 1-0 to Hearts and those of us who think of the pint glass as being half empty rather than half full assured ourselves that at least there would be no repeat of the scoreline of New Years Day.

Hearts had looked confident from kick-off but the goal gave another surge to the adrenaline. Hibs were forced to back-pedal as Ford and Busby came close to adding to the score with Jim Jefferies proving to be an unlikely threat with his crosses. It was all Hearts and the only concern as the referee blew his whistle for half time was that Hearts had managed only one goal.

Hibs manager Eddie Turnbull knew things had to change and he replaced former Hearts star Alan Gordon with Tony Higgins and Alex Edwards with Ian Munro at the start of the second half. Then it rained goals! In the 54th minute, Kenny Aird set off down the right wing with the Hibs defence chasing. At the edge of the penalty box, the former St. Johnstone man fired in a shot that slipped under the body of the hapless McKenzie and Hearts were 2-0 ahead. Those of us in maroon and white went wild. Aird had promised much since his arrival in Edinburgh and scoring against Hibs made him an instant hero.

But, just as we began our songs of praise, Hibs raced to the other end of the park and pulled a goal back. This time it was Hearts keeper Kenny Garland who was the victim of a misunderstanding with Jimmy Cant leaving Alex Cropley to flick the ball into the net. But, remarkably, within seconds, 2-1 for Hearts became 3-1. John Stevenson ran at a startled Hibs defence and was through on goalkeeper McKenzie. The Hibs number one brought Stevenson crashing to the ground – only for the ball to break to Donald Ford. The striker, who would end the season being named in Scotland's World Cup squad for the finals in Munich, thrashed the ball into the net to send the Hearts support delirious once more.

It had been three minutes of bedlam and Hearts, with their two goal advantage instantly restored, sensed revenge for the events of January 1st. Ford and Busby continued to wreak havoc and Hearts twice struck the crossbar as Hibs tried manfully to stem the maroon tide.

Keeper McKenzie redeemed himself for his earlier mistakes by producing some fine saves, as, with the New Year hangover showing signs of lifting at last (not for me of course, being just eleven years old – honest, officer!) Hearts fans demanded their favourites go for the kill. With just ten minutes left, Hearts got the fourth goal their play so richly deserved. Thirty yards out the man with one of the most fearsome shots in Scottish football – Drew Busby – let fly with a screamer. McKenzie's day of misery was complete when he allowed the ball to slip under his body and into the net. 4-1 for Hearts and Drew Busby had opened his Tynecastle scoring account in the best possible manner.

Those Hibs fans who had taunted us on their last visit to Gorgie – and at every opportunity since – were now streaming for the exits, praying that the memory of that occasion wouldn't be tarnished by a thumping win for Hearts. They were thankful that the scoring ended at 4-1 and the maroon half of Tynecastle loudly acclaimed their side at the final whistle. A team which had barely managed a goal a game the season before had opened the centenary season with seven in two games and had thrashed their rivals into the bargain.

Hearts fans spilled out on to Gorgie Road after the game in high spirits. They had criticised the manager and the board of directors for not spending enough money on bringing quality players to Tynecastle. Now, at last, money had been spent – and, on this early evidence, wisely. Kenny Aird and John Stevenson looked talented players who could stretch any defence while the fans had a new striking hero to acclaim. For years Donald Ford had been something of a lone figure up front in maroon. Now Drew Busby looked to be the answer to a long-standing problem and Hearts fans everywhere looked forward to a genuine challenge for the league championship. The striker's name became immortalised in the chant 'His name is Drew Busby, he comes from the north, he plays at Tynecastle, just over the Forth, he drinks all your whisky and Newcastle Brown, the Gorgie Boys are in town........nah, nah, nah' etc. etc. Now I'm sure the line about Super Drew's drinking habits wasn't accurate but it sounded good on the Tynecastle terracing!

Buoyed by this impressive start, Hearts embarked on an unbeaten run that lasted until the end of October – and took them to the top of the league. This run included a highly impressive 3-0 victory over Rangers at Ibrox – the Gers heaviest home defeat for a decade – and there was phenomenal interest when Celtic visited Tynecastle on October 27th 1973. It was a top of the table clash in every sense. Over 35,000 fans packed into Tynecastle but most left disappointed as Jock Stein's impressive side won 3-1 and in doing so knocked Hearts from the top of the league. It was to prove a defining moment of the season. Shortly afterwards Hearts lost 5-0 to Burnley in a Texaco Cup tie and the noise of the players confidence crashing to earth was deafening. After a 1-1 draw with Dundee United, Hearts then lost 3-1 at Aberdeen and hopes of a centenary league championship began to fade.

Hearts finished season 1973-74 in joint sixth place, fifteen points behind the champions. With title hopes disappearing, Hearts supporters turned to the Scottish Cup for the last chance of glory. After Clyde were beaten 3-1 at Tynecastle, things looked bleak when Partick Thistle grabbed a 1-1 draw in Gorgie thus forcing a replay at Firhill. However there were signs of the early season sparkle returning to Hearts play when they thrashed

Thistle 4-1 in the replay and so faced Ayr United in the quarter final. It was almost a repeat performance. Hearts struggled to a 1-1 draw at Tynecastle before winning the replay at Somerset Park 2-1 to reach their first cup semi-final in six years. Hearts got the draw they wanted by avoiding Celtic and were paired with Dundee United. After another disappointing 1-1 draw at Hampden Park, the teams returned to Mount Florida three days later where United won the replay 4-2 on a night of crushing disappointment for all Hearts supporters. Strangely, I felt the pain of losing that semi-final almost as much as the 7-0 defeat from Hibernian. Being stuck in the Granite City, I couldn't get to Hampden for the midweek game but I was certain I would get to the national stadium for the final – my first cup final. I had already been on to my father with instructions to make sure he got cup final tickets. It was an early, painful lesson that you can never, ever take anything for granted if you're a Hearts supporter.

1974 also saw Scotland begin their tradition of 'gallant losers' in the World Cup. Willie Ormond's men – including Donald Ford – returned unbeaten from West Germany having beaten Zaire and drawn with Brazil and Yugoslavia. But, not for the first time, the Scots went out on goal difference. Many Hearts fans doubted the wisdom of playing an ageing Denis Law in the opening game against Zaire when Fordie would have surely been more of a threat up front.

Everyone bar Celtic fans had become bored rigid with Jock Stein's side winning league championships with monotonous regularity. Even the Scottish League were beginning to get fed up and so Scottish league football was revolutionised in 1975 with the advent of the Premier

Division. The plan was to have a ten club top division with the teams playing each other four times a season. The idea was that this would make Scottish football more competitive – no more fixtures at the end of April against Arbroath to decide if you'll finish eleventh in the league or twelfth.

So in season 1974-75, it was decided that the top ten teams in the then eighteen team First Division would form the new Premier League the following season. Nae bother for Hearts eh? What was I saying about taking things for granted? Hearts began the league season with a 2-1 defeat by St. Johnstone at Tynecastle and did not win a league game until the end of October. This catastrophic start included results such as a 4-1 defeat by Aberdeen at Tynecastle, another 4-1 thumping from Partick Thistle at Firhill and a 5-0 hammering from Dundee United at Tannadice. As November beckoned, Hearts were struggling at the foot of the table and a place in the top ten seemed a forlorn hope even at this stage. Bobby Seith appeased many Hearts fans by tendering his resignation. John Hagart was appointed as his replacement, initially until the end of the season. With no money to spend on new players, Hagart was being asked to perform a miracle – and he nearly did. He brought in Don Murray from Cardiff City on a free transfer, made a couple of tactical changes and the effect on Hearts was immediate. From being bottom of the league, the Gorgie Boys embarked on a fifteen game unbeaten run that only ended with a 2-1 defeat by Rangers at Ibrox. Hearts sneaked into the top ten at the end of the season – they finished eighth, just four points ahead of eleventh placed Airdrieonians. It had been a close call, too close for comfort but an ominous sign of what lay in store for

Hearts supporters as the decade that taste forgot progressed.

If the new Premier League was meant to herald a new, exciting age in Scottish football, then someone forgot to mention this at Tynecastle. In the space of fifteen years, Hearts had slipped from champions of Scotland to mid-table mediocrity. If Hearts struggled in the middle of the old First Division, how would they fare in a league of ten, having to face the Old Firm four times a season? And two trips to Easter Road where they hadn't won since the halcyon days of the early 1960s. The answer was soon apparent – badly.

In August 1975 the Premier League era began auspiciously for Hearts when they lost the first game 1-0 at Easter Road and, while there were eight teams fewer in the new league, the fare on offer remained mediocre. St. Johnstone soon became detached at the bottom of the league but the Scottish League, in their infinite wisdom, had decided that two clubs would face relegation at the season's end. On the less than wild assumption that neither of the Old Firm would struggle in the lower reaches of the league, this meant in reality that a quarter of the Premier Division would be relegated. Inevitably, Hearts were involved in the battle to avoid the drop but a crucial 3-0 hammering of Aberdeen at Pittodrie in April 1976 meant wiped brows for Jambos everywhere. Hearts were superb that night with Ralph Callachan producing a masterful display in midfield. The Dons themselves were facing the ignominy of the drop but the arrival of Ally MacLeod as their manager turned things around and they defeated Hibernian 3-0 on the last day of the season to save their bacon. It was Dundee who joined St. Johnstone on the downward spiral to Division One but I wasn't the only nervous Hearts supporter who thought calamity was just around the corner.

Alleviating the pain of the sometimes tortuous process of league survival was a Scottish Cup run that is still talked about today by ageing Jambos like myself over a foaming pint of eighty shillings in The Diggers. After less than enthralling victories over Clyde and Stirling Albion, Hearts were drawn to face Montrose at Links Park. A great draw for me, still living in Aberdeen in 1976, as it was just a forty-five minute train journey from the Granite City. Montrose were one of the leading lights in the First Division in the mid 1970s and had famously knocked Hibernian out of the League Cup that same season. Cue media clichés about capital doubles, capital punishment etc. Sure enough, Hearts struggled on a tight pitch and trailed 2-1 well into injury time. I headed for the exit with tears in my eyes – how could this team of mine do this to me? Fighting relegation was bad enough but to lose to a pokey little northern team for whom the 8,000 crowd was their biggest for years (and 6,000 of them were Hearts fans) was disastrous. Cue Graham 'Shuggie' Shaw to find space in the penalty box in the dying seconds and scramble the ball into the net for the equaliser. 2-2 and scenes of joy I had never witnessed yet as a Hearts fan.

I wasn't at the replay at Tynecastle but, naturally, Hearts having convinced the fans they had done the hard bit, promptly went two goals down within half an hour. With collective blood pressure rising, the maroons came storming back to make it 2-2 but extra time ended with the scores still level. In the days of the innocent seventies, the Scottish Football Association didn't believe in penalty shoot-outs and so a second replay was ordered.

Not at Tynecastle or Links Park you understand – it was at Muirton Park, Perth meaning both sets of fans had to travel a considerable distance in midweek. Another ninety minutes – another draw, this time 1-1. At this rate it looked like the Scottish Cup final would have to be delayed until July. But, silky Ralph Callachan scored a goal in extra time to edge Hearts through 2-1 and a Hampden semi-final beckoned once more.

When Hearts were drawn against yet another First Division side – Dumbarton – those journalistic hacks who like to think of themselves as knowledgeable were already writing the programme notes for a Rangers v. Hearts final. Those of us with mental scars of following Edinburgh's finest knew the truth – yet another draw occurred, a truly awful goalless affair with the Sons of the Rock. Thankfully, Hearts improved for the replay – they couldn't have played any worse – and a Walter Smith own goal (yes, that Walter Smith) put John Hagart's men on the way to a 3-0 victory and Hearts first Scottish Cup Final appearance in eight years.

It was Rangers in the final. And Hearts began the game as only they could – they were a goal down before three o'clock. Referee R. H. Davidson blew for kick-off at two minutes to three and within sixty seconds, Rangers had scored. It ended 3-1 for Jock Wallace's side with Shuggie Shaw inevitably scoring for Hearts. Another huge Hampden disappointment – as you will know by the end of this book, Hearts don't win at Mount Florida very often.

Still, we had the taste of the cup final and we all wanted more. John Hagart had done a reasonable job as manager up to this point and Hearts certainly began season 1976-77 in impressive fashion, putting the likes of

Motherwell, Dundee and Partick Thistle to the sword in the League Cup.

But, not for the first time, fate was waiting in a dark alley for Hearts – and wearing steel toe-capped boots...........

3

The Rollercoaster Begins
1976-1983

The Dynamic Duo -
John Robertson & Sandy Clark

1976-1983

TEENAGE YEARS can be quite traumatic. For the traumatised parents, I mean. I have two teenage daughters who drive me up the wall but I love them dearly (dearly being the operative word). I was 14 in 1976 and giving my poor, demented mother a hard time. In my defence, my hormones were akin to the Hearts back four of the time – all over the place. And following Hearts only added to my angst.

The inaugural season of the Premier Division had been a nervous affair for Hearts supporters but, for once, I was hopeful. The Scottish Cup Final had whetted the appetite for Hearts to at least get close to something tangible and it genuinely appeared, in the summer of 1976, that manager John Hagart had transformed Hearts from a team barely worthy of Premier Division status to a team capable of challenging Rangers and Celtic. Everyone knew what the new Premier Division was about after its first season – survival. Dundee and St. Johnstone had failed to survive that first season and were replaced by Kilmarnock and Partick Thistle. The previous season had been too close for comfort but surely a rejuvenated Hearts would have no worries? And season 1976-77 had the additional pleasure of the maroons in European competition for the first time in fourteen years, thanks to Rangers having completed the domestic treble, thereby allowing Hearts – as Scottish Cup runners-up – to enter the European Cup Winners Cup. To a teenage Jambo like myself this was unchartered territory but when the draw paired Hearts with the crack East German side Locomotive Leipzig, my heart sank. If Hearts required three games to dispose of pesky Montrose, how would they fare against one of Europe's top sides (as Leipzig were in the mid 1970s)?

As usual, the season began with the League Cup and Hearts started in impressive fashion, particularly when they thrashed Motherwell 4-1 at Fir Park. Remarkably, given the JTs woeful record in this competition since they last lifted the trophy in 1962, Hearts won the section that also included demoted Dundee and promoted Partick Thistle. This meant a two-legged quarter final tie against First Division Falkirk – who had knocked Hearts out at the same stage two seasons earlier. But Hagart's boys thrashed the Bairns (sorry – I've tried to avoid clichés like the plague – there goes another one!- but I just couldn't help myself) 4-1 at Tynecastle and while the return at Brockville was lost 4-3, Hearts were through to yet another last four appearance at Hampden on a 7-5 aggregate. Inevitably, the Old Firm avoided each other in the semi-final draw and Hearts were paired with Celtic. Despite a spirited showing, a late Kenny Dalgleish goal gave Jock Stein's side a 2-1 win. In the other semi-final, Aberdeen didn't just ignore the script, they tore it to shreds and did the same to Rangers defence – they hammered the Gers 5-1 and went on to beat Celtic in the final. I was at Linksfield Academy's school disco on the evening of the game (for those readers under the age of twenty, ask your parents what disco means) and when the DJ aka the school's Teacher of Art announced the final score was 5-1 to Aberdeen I worried about the influence of alcohol on society.....

Hearts began the league campaign with a series of draws. The opening fixture was handy for me although, arriving late, I missed Drew Busby scoring Hearts first league goal of the season after just thirty seconds at Pittodrie. I sat through the game believing Hearts were losing but the final score ended up 2-2. While further draws ensued and one felt it would be nice to get a few wins under our belt, Hearts fans were happy with their team's start to the season and their contentment turned to elation when the Cup Winner's Cup tie came around. Hearts had played reasonably well in the first leg in East Germany but lost, rather unluckily, 2-0 meaning it would be a huge task to overturn the deficit in the return at Tynecastle. But on a balmy September evening in Gorgie, Hearts produced a performance that is still talked about in pubs and clubs by those of a maroon persuasion today. More than 18,000 Hearts fans packed Tynecastle hoping for the early goal that would catapult John Hagart's men back into the tie. With an atmosphere that sent shivers down the back of the neck, Hearts threw players into attack from the off and such adventurous play had overturned the two goal deficit by half an hour thanks to goals by Roy Kay and Willie Gibson. Leipzig didn't know what hit them and the Hearts fans could scarcely believe that their team, who hadn't won a league game thus far, were taking one of East Germany's finest teams apart. But, as so often happens in European ties, it took just one slip of concentration to prove costly. Just before half-time, Leipzig hit Hearts on the break and a sweeping move saw them score. Not only were the East Germans now back in front on aggregate but they had scored an away goal which would count as double if the aggregate score was level at the end of the night.

Tynecastle was stunned. Hearts had been so impressive in that first half but it looked as if their efforts would count for nothing. They would have to score another two goals in the second half to progress. Remarkably, Hearts began the second forty-five minutes the way they began the first – on the offensive. Urged on by a passionate support, unaccustomed to big nights of European football, Hearts swarmed forward again. Jim Brown scored to level the aggregate scores and, with Tynecastle in a frenzy, Drew Busby scored Hearts fourth goal. Willie Gibson capped a magnificent night by adding a fifth near the end to make the final score Hearts 5 Locomotive Leipzig 1. The fans could scarcely believe it. It was a result and a performance that made Europe sit up and take note. Leipzig were touted by many as one of the favourites for the competition and the fact they were taken apart by a team that couldn't score against Dumbarton five months previously was nothing short of startling. The more excitable among the Hearts support were thinking of the JTs being among the favourites to go on and lift the trophy. Although just fourteen at the time, I had already experienced enough of the ways of following Edinburgh's finest to realise this would be fantasy stuff. Hearts were drawn with West German opposition in the second round in the shape of SV Hamburg but comparisons with the non-communist and communist German leagues was fanciful to say the least. West Germany were World Cup holders in 1976 (although they had unexpectedly lost their European Championship crown that summer to Czechoslovakia) and Hamburg had serious designs on winning the

Bundesliga. They were less than a year away from one of the transfer sensations of the decade – the capture of Kevin Keegan from Liverpool in 1977 made headlines around the world – and it was clear Hamburg were a step up in class from Leipzig. Nevertheless, Hearts put up another spirited performance in the first leg in West Germany and an injury time goal from Donald Park saw John Hagart's men return to Edinburgh with a 4-2 defeat. Almost a thrashing – but Hearts had scored two away goals to give the fans real hope of another spectacular comeback in Gorgie for the second leg. Over 25,000 supporters packed into Tynecastle hoping for another European glory night. But it wasn't to be. Hamburg scored a crucial early goal and you could almost see the Hearts team deflate. The fighting spirit that had typified the victory over Leipzig was replaced by a cold-blooded realism that Hamburg had effectively killed the tie with that early goal. A hushed Tynecastle watched a masterclass performance by the West Germans who went on to win 4-1 on the night, for a humiliating 8-3 aggregate victory. Willie Gibson was again the Hearts goalscorer.

The cracks in Hearts confidence began to deepen. Out of two cup competitions in a matter of weeks, the turning point of Hearts season – and of this great club's history – came on November 20th when Celtic visited Tynecastle for a league match. In an extraordinary game, Willie Gibson had the game of his life and scored a first-half hat-trick as Hearts raced to a 3-1 half-time lead. It was a marvellous performance, not only by Gibbie but the whole Hearts team. But in the second half – calamity. Celtic displayed the spirit for which they have become renowned and stormed back with three second half goals to win the game 4-3. After the Hamburg nightmare, this was a defining moment for Hearts. The early season swagger and style disappeared after the Celtic game. It was replaced by nervous, debilitating performances as confidence was shot to pieces. And in the new cut throat Premier League, showing signs of weakness was a perilous trait.

Hearts lost to Rangers and Partick Thistle in quick succession and nerves began to fray. John Hagart's men were in mid-table but the nature of the Premier League meant a couple of bad results saw you plunge down the table. A crushing 4-1 defeat from Aberdeen at Pittodrie on January 3rd got 1977 off to a bad start. I couldn't believe how poor Hearts were that day. It was 4-1 going on 8-1. The month of February seemed to epitomise Hearts season. We all thought the corner had been turned when Hearts raced into a four goal lead by half-time against Kilmarnock at Tynecastle and while the final score remained 4-0, Hearts fans believed their team was on the way back at last. But, just two days later, Hearts were thumped 5-1 by Celtic at Parkhead and, worse, just ten days after the 4-0 win over Killie, Hearts slumped to a 2-1 defeat in a re-arranged match at Rugby Park. That was a defining moment for me. In my heart of hearts, I knew Hearts were going down. Relegation had never happened to this great club before but it looked inevitable from that day on. Kilmarnock had scarcely won a game all season and were already doomed. Ayr United were Hearts main rivals in the bid to avoid the drop. The Honest Men came to Tynecastle for the proverbial 'four-pointer' as it was in those days. Hearts had to win to close the gap that had opened up between the two clubs. But Ayr won 2-1 on a woeful midweek night, a game reminiscent of when Hearts lost the league championship to Kilmarnock in 1965. Hearts lost to both the Old Firm at Tynecastle within a week and the last Edinburgh derby of the season – and who knew for how long – attracted barely 11,000 punters to Gorgie. Hearts came from behind to salvage a 2-2 draw but few cared. Hearts, Hearts, Glorious Hearts were relegated and condemned to a season – at least – in the First Division. More than a decade of neglect had come to a head.

Hearts reached the semi-finals of both the Scottish Cup and League Cup but lost to Rangers and Celtic. It would be more than a year until they met the Old Firm again. Inevitably, John Hagart left Tynecastle and his replacement caused something of a shock for the whole of Scottish football. Scotland manager Willie Ormond left the hot seat at Park Gardens citing the reason that he missed the day-to-day involvement of club football. Ormond had built a fine Scotland team and his appointment at Tynecastle was seen by many as an ambitious move. Not so by some Hearts fans who regarded a man who was a member of Hibernian's Famous Five forward line of the 1950s with more than a hint of suspicion.

Nonetheless, Hearts supporters got behind the team in increasing numbers for life in the First Division when season 1977-78 began with a trip to the west coast Riviera that was Boghead where Hearts drew 2-2 with Dumbarton. Defeat by Hamilton Academicals at Tynecastle and Montrose at Links Park confirmed what most of us had already surmised – the job of getting out of the backwater that was First Division football was not going to be easy. Consecutive defeats from Kilmarnock – yes, them again – and East Fife saw the Gorgie natives get restless. Scarcely a year had passed since that great European victory over Leipzig – now there was a Hibby in charge and Hearts couldn't even top the First Division.

But the team rallied and embarked on an unbeaten run that lasted from mid November until the end of the season. Hearts tanked Arbroath 7-0 at Gayfield just before Christmas, and then their bogey team – and contenders for promotion – Kilmarnock 3-0 at Tynecastle. With Morton holding a clear lead at the top of the league it looked like the second promotion place would be between Hearts and Dundee. When the two met at Tynecastle in early January 1978, the game attracted a record crowd for the First Division – 19,700. The game ended 2-2 but Hearts belated impressive form saw them grind out results when it mattered and the maroons clinched promotion with a 1-0 win over Arbroath at Gayfield on the last day of the season. Eammon Bannon headed the only goal in front of 6,000 travelling Hearts fans who invaded the pitch at the final whistle. Hearts were back! But not for long...

It was obvious to everyone that the team that had almost made such a fist of getting promotion would be nowhere near good enough for the cut throat Premier League. And so it proved. As the much anticipated 1978/79 season kicked off, 11,000 fans turned up at Tynecastle for Hearts opening game on their return to the big time – and they saw Aberdeen canter to a 4-1 win. A 4-0 thrashing from Celtic followed seven days later. Action had to be taken. It was. But few of us could understand it. Willie Ormond traded one of Hearts best players – Donald Park – for two Partick Thistle reserve players, Denis McQuade and John Craig. The fans couldn't believe it. Apart from a three week spell in

November when Hearts signed striker Derek O'Connor and defeated Celtic, Aberdeen and Hibernian, the Gorgie Boys looked second-rate material. A familiar tale throughout this book has been the sale of a crucial player at a crucial time for Hearts. January 1979 saw Eammon Bannon head for Chelsea for £200,000. It appeased an increasingly fraught bank manager but directed Hearts to the exit door of the Premier League once again. Willie Ormond's team lost their final ten league games on the bounce, eight of which they failed to score. Relegated again. Humiliated once more. A record in the charts of the day was Lynsey de Paul's 'Rock Bottom'. That was sung to me on more than one occasion by heartless Aberdonians. 'Where are Hearts? Rock Bottom'. And I couldn't argue with the sentiments.

It was back to life in the First Division and Hearts began season 1979-80 with five straight wins but no one was being fooled this time. Manager Ormond tried to mix youth and experience but ageing players such as Bobby Robinson and Jim Denny had their best years behind them. Fans heroes, Drew Busby and Rab Prentice had left Tynecastle under a cloud and their replacements were players the fans had never heard of. The standard of the First Division that season was poor, which meant that Hearts could top the league even with sub-standard performances. But draws with Berwick Rangers, Dumbarton and Clyde were sair tae bair. The end was in sight for manager Willie Ormond and the end of the line came when Hearts threw away a three goal lead against Clydebank at Tynecastle and ended up with a draw. It was January 5th 1980. A time when the crowds traditionally pack the terraces. Barely 5,000 came to Tynecastle. Although Hearts were top of the league,

Ormond was sacked. His replacement was former Newcastle and Scotland centre half Bobby Moncur – and he had four months to get it right.

With the club in desperate financial trouble, Moncur knew he would get no money to spend on new players. He scrambled Hearts across the finishing line for promotion with the existing squad and even landed Hearts the First Division championship with a final day win over Airdrieonians at Tynecastle. But the punters knew the score. Moncur led Hearts to the quarter finals of the Scottish Cup and faced Rangers at Ibrox. Incredibly, Hearts took the lead through a Tom Forsyth own goal in the opening minute. It gave Hearts a cash prize from the sponsors for the quickest goal of the competition. Had Bobby Moncur worked a miracle? Erm, no. Rangers won 6-1. As the song goes, there may be trouble ahead...

If Bobby Moncur did anything for Hearts it was to transform its youth policy. When I say transform, Hearts didn't really have a youth policy before Moncur arrived. He signed a clutch of talented kids on the premise of that if they're good enough they're old enough. The best of them would get their chance in the first team sooner than anticipated. As Hearts began season 1980-81 back in the Premier Division with defeat at Partick Thistle, Moncur brought in former Rangers, Celtic and Tottenham player Alfie Conn. Older Hearts fans shook their collective heads. Conn's father, of course, had been an integral part of the all-conquering Hearts team of the 1950s. Conn Junior, by now some way past his best, didn't look as if he could lace his father's boots. After encouraging wins over St. Mirren and Kilmarnock, the predictable slump followed. Hearts won just one of their next twenty two games. In despair, manager Moncur introduced youngsters Paul O'Brien, Alex Hamill, David Bowman and Gary Mackay. Only Bowman and Mackay looked the part. Alex MacDonald was signed from Rangers but had little effect. Relegation was a reality from day one and was finally confirmed in early spring. Moncur was offered the manager's job at Plymouth Argyle and you could hardly see him for the dust. His assistant Tony Ford took over.

Hearts debts reached a critical stage. A third relegation in four years had the financial vultures hovering over Tynecastle, as the death knell was about to sound for one of Scottish football's great institutions. I couldn't believe what was happening. No Hearts fan could. Sensing catastrophe, former Hearts striker Donald Ford, by now an accountant of some calibre, persuaded property tycoon Wallace Mercer to plough more than £350,000 into the club to save it from closure. Against his better judgement at the time, Mercer wrote a cheque that saved Hearts for the time being.

It was with much angst that we stood on the Tynecastle terracings in August 1981 to witness Hearts embark on yet another season in the First Division. I had nothing but feelings of despair and was desperate for anything to take my mind off the perilous state my beloved Heart of Midlothian was in. I even got engaged to be married – I was looking for any excuse not to go to Tynecastle on a Saturday! I was still living in Aberdeen at that time so my trips to Gorgie were more infrequent that season than any other. I wasn't alone. Less than 3,500 turned up at Tynecastle to see Hearts defeat Hamilton Academicals. And Hearts displays had become desperate. Tony Ford's tactics were bizarre to say the least. The ageing Peter Marinello had signed and, being a

Hibernian pin-up boy from the late 1960s, was hardly a favourite in Gorgie. Mercer's cash injection gave the manager some cash to spend on players and he signed former Scotland striker Willie Pettigrew and Derek Addison from Dundee United for a combined fee of £180,000. That was an astonishing fee. Hearts had suddenly gone from near bankruptcy to splashing out a record transfer fee. Few of us knew that Hearts had agreed to pay the fee over a period of time – years as it turned out! But still Hearts struggled. When Hearts could only manage a draw with Queens Park in December, Wallace Mercer – having spent a small fortune on saving the club – lost patience. He sacked the anonymous Ford and gave the coaching duties to Alex MacDonald until the end of the season. With Hearts in turmoil, the club's most embarrassing result in nearly 110 years occurred when Second Division Forfar Athletic won a Scottish Cup tie 1-0 at Tynecastle in February 1982.

Legendary journalist and renowned Jambo, John Fairgrieve wrote in the Sunday Mail the following day that Hearts should close and Tynecastle be turned into a car park. Heartbroken, we echoed his sentiments. How much more suffering could we take? And all my fiancé could talk about was the bloody wedding!

But Alex MacDonald rallied his troops. With his inspired leadership, Hearts won seven league games on the trot and suddenly, against all odds, promotion was a possibility. Motherwell, with youngsters Brian McClair and Gary McAllister pulling the strings, were so far ahead at the top of the league, they had secured promotion some time before. Second place was the target for Hearts – and for old rivals Kilmarnock. Hearts had eased themselves into second place and were 2-1 up at half-time against Dumbarton at Tynecastle in the third last game of the season. Then, disaster struck once more. The Sons proved themselves to be the men of the day, scored four second half goals and won 5-2. The 4,800 Hearts fans turned on MacDonald and his team. The walls were about to come tumbling down on Hearts promotion bid. A goalless draw with Kilmarnock the following week meant Hearts had to avoid defeat at home to Motherwell on the final day of the season to scrape promotion. They also had a superior goal difference of five goals. The script, though, was painfully familiar. Hearts lost 1-0. Kilmarnock had already raced to a 6-0 lead against relegated Queen of the South at half-time. Killie up – Hearts faced with a second successive season in the First Division. Crowd trouble broke out at Tynecastle. Several arrests were made. Wallace Mercer even came into the old Tynecastle shed to plead with the fans to behave. Anger, frustration and, above all, hurt engulfed the bitter supporters. Hearts faced the real prospect of part-time football. Wallace Mercer and his beleaguered board of directors spent the summer restructuring the finances of a once proud club. Hearts would remain full-time for one more season. But promotion to the Premier Division simply had to be achieved in season 1982-83. Alex MacDonald was appointed manager on a permanent basis. He gutted the playing staff and brought in ex Rangers colleagues Sandy Jardine and Willie Johnston. Jardine, with a wealth of experience, was made assistant manager.

As if I hadn't been emotionally drained enough in 1982, there was also the World Cup to endure in Spain. Scotland, led by Jock Stein, started with a bang, defeating New Zealand 5-2. Then, it all went wrong (stop me if you've heard this before). The Scots faced the favourites for the tournament, a Zico inspired Brazil. Dundee United's David Narey scored a peach of a goal – famously described by English commentator Jimmy Hill as a 'toe-poke' – and we dreamed of a famous victory. The dream didn't last long. Brazil went on to win 4-1. As goalkeeper Alan Rough watched another Brazilian shot float over his permed head and into the net, I was thoroughly depressed. I was getting married the day after. My beloved knew what she was letting herself in for by marrying a manic Hearts supporter who puts the Gorgie Boys ahead of all else. We're still together after twenty odd years but she has threatened divorce on more than one occasion as a result of my devotion to Edinburgh's finest. 'On what grounds?' I asked. 'Oh, Tynecastle, Easter Road, Pittodrie…….' Anyway, in Scotland's next game, the central defensive partnership of Willie Miller and Alan Hansen collided with each other to allow the Soviet Union to score a comic cuts goal and while Graeme Souness equalised for the Scots, the 2-2 draw meant Scotland were out in the first round again.

Strangely, given the events of May 1982, there was an optimistic air around Tynecastle as Hearts began season 1982-83 with a 2-1 win over Queens Park at Hampden. The young brigade had another, notable recruit. Fresh faced seventeen year old striker John Robertson, whose brother Chris had played for Hearts the season before. Hearts lost just one of their opening dozen games and Alex MacDonald had the team playing with the heart (you wouldn't expect a book like this not to have a pun like that somewhere?!) Hearts even reached the semi-finals of the League Cup where they lost a two-legged affair to Rangers. In the first leg at Ibrox there was the clearest sign yet that MacDonald and Jardine were getting it right. Hearts held Rangers to a goalless draw until the last ten minutes when Rangers superior fitness saw them score two late goals. 19,000 witnessed the return leg at Tynecastle and while Hearts lost that 2-1, the fans were encouraged. They were also encouraged – and enraged – with Hearts performance against Celtic at Parkhead in the Scottish Cup. MacDonald's side were more than holding their own when Willie Johnston was controversially sent off after a tussle with Celtic's Davie Provan. Johnston protests his innocence to this day – even Wallace Mercer wrote to the Scottish Football Association to plead his case. Hearts lost 4-1 amid a sense of huge injustice.

On the brighter side, young John Robertson was introduced to the team on a regular basis in the New Year and it was clear here was a star in the making. Robbo scored 16 goals in 14 appearances and Alex MacDonald just couldn't leave him out. Hearts duly achieved promotion with a team that held more promise than other maroon teams in a decade.

Hearts were back again. This time for good. And the Gorgie Boys were about to dispel six years of gloom with performances that would light up the Premier League!

4

Back Among the Big Boys
1983-1985

Sandy Clark

1983-1985

AUGUST 1983. I had served fourteen months of my life sentence i.e. marriage to Mrs Smith. I didn't feel too bad. My mate was gutted though. He had returned from a week in Holland having looked forward to being 'entertained' by Amsterdam Annie, a Dutch lady who performed great tricks with a pair of inflatable Dutch shoes. But my pal looked glum on his return to Aberdeen. Amsterdam Annie was no more. Apparently she had popped her clogs.....

After two long years, Heart of Midlothian FC were back in the top flight of Scottish football. A club of this standing should never have been away in the first place. Nerves were fraught. After suffering three relegations in five seasons, no one dared to presume Hearts would get it right at last. But one could sense there was a new spirit about Tynecastle. The old guard had gone, those who were guilty of mismanagement had been shown the door and a new team both on and off the field was taking shape. Chairman Wallace Mercer had only been in charge for a couple of years but he had already shown he would not suffer fools gladly. He courted the media with some style, believing that anything that would bring Hearts to the public's attention could be turned into something positive.

Football was changing in the 1980s. And for this

Hearts supporter, life had changed too. Gone were the single, carefree days replaced by marital status, a mortgage and added responsibilities. I was still living in Aberdeen when Hearts returned to the Premier Division and I was ribbed constantly about the status of the two clubs at the time. In May 1983, Aberdeen defeated Real Madrid to lift the European Cup Winners Cup and still had a chance of lifting the League championship the following Saturday. All roads lead to Pittodrie screamed the local press but not for me. I was at Tynecastle to see Hearts defeat Hamilton Academicals 2-0 on the final day of the league season. While cocky Aberdonians sneered that this was Hearts biggest game of the season, I was content that Hearts had a better chance of surviving the rigours of the Premier League than at any time before.

Manager Alex MacDonald knew the painful lessons of previous promoted Hearts teams had to be learnt. There was an obvious gulf in the standard of play between the First and Premier Divisions. Money was still too tight to mention at Tynecastle but MacDonald knew the players he wanted to bring in. Players with Premier League experience, who knew how to scrap for survival. Hearts aim for season 1983-84 was to finish eighth in the league table, thus avoiding relegation. Young striker John Robertson had been a revelation in the second half of the promotion season but many doubted whether the youngster rejected by Hibernian would be able to handle the step up in class. Alex MacDonald surprised many by bringing in the highly experienced Jimmy Bone as wee Robbo's strike partner. Bone may have been in the twilight of a long career that had seen a tour of duty with Partick Thistle, Celtic, Norwich, Arbroath and Hong Kong among others but he was the ideal man to show

Robertson the ropes of playing in the Premier League. MacDonald also brought back fans favourite Donald Park from Firhill and signed former Scotland youth cap George Cowie from West Ham. The team was almost unrecognisable from the Hearts side that last appeared in the Premier League in the spring of 1981 and with the likes of MacDonald, Sandy Jardine, Willie Johnston and Stewart MacLaren playing alongside Jimmy Bone, the predictable media corps labelled the Hearts side Dad's Army, conveniently forgetting the team also had teenagers Robertson, Davie Bowman and Gary Mackay.

As always seemed to be the case, the Scottish League's fixture computer gave Hearts an away fixture for their opening game back in the Premier League. But it was against promotion bedfellows St. Johnstone and the critics immediately tagged the game as the first relegation battle of the season. Another huge Hearts travelling support headed for Muirton Park and witnessed a scrappy affair. Even in the first game of the season, the tension was evident. A goalless draw looked on the cards until Jimmy Bone let rip from twenty-five yards out with a rasping shot, which flew into the net. It was enough to give Hearts a 1-0 victory; an unusual occurrence for the first league game of the season and its importance was not under-estimated. The Perth Saints were faced with games against Celtic, Rangers, Aberdeen and Dundee United in succession and the Hearts faithful sensed their team could build up an early points advantage over the team who pipped them for the First Division championship a few weeks before. And wipe the smile from the cheeky Saints programme editor who ribbed Hearts about where the First Division Championship flag was flying.

The League Cup took centre stage the following week and a dire performance against Cowdenbeath – Hearts required penalties to secure victory after a goalless draw at Tynecastle – was notable for only one thing. The performance of the Blue Brazil's towering centre half was exceptional and he seemed to be waging a one-man defence against the Hearts attack. Cowdenbeath's Craig Levein's reward for such an impressive performance was a return trip to Tynecastle a few weeks later – to sign for Hearts. A decision that would have huge implications for this young man later in life.

Next up was a fixture that had been sorely missed for four years – the Edinburgh derby. Hearts hadn't played Hibernian since 1979 as, when Hearts were promoted in 1980, the wee team were heading in the opposite direction to the First Division. 20,000 headed for Tynecastle – Hearts biggest home attendance in five years – to witness one of the great derby games. Hibs looked in control early on and took the lead through former Hearts man Ralph Callachan (it pained this Hearts fan to see such a talented player play for the Hibees) The omens didn't look good for Hearts and Hibs looked like they were going to add to their score. At half-time only one goal separated the sides but, standing in the old enclosure at the front of the main stand, I felt uneasy. Hearts seemed non-existent in midfield. Manager Alex MacDonald clearly felt the same early in the second half and he brought himself on to replace Gary Mackay. The transformation was almost immediate. Two minutes later, Hearts equalised with one of the best goals ever scored in an Edinburgh derby – and it proved to be the first of a derby record for John Robertson. Hearts keeper Henry Smith launched the ball forward and with wind assistance it fell at the feet of eighteen-year-old Robertson. With a breathtaking piece of skill rarely seen by Hearts fans since the golden age of the 1950s, Robbo controlled the ball with his right foot, turned Hibs veteran Arthur Duncan, spotted Hibs keeper Alan Rough off his line and curled a magnificent left foot shot past the startled permed one. 1-1. It was one of those goals that remained etched on the memory and fans in Gorgie who saw it still talk about it to this day.

It set the derby alight and those of us on the crumbling Tynecastle terracing celebrated wildly. But the celebrations didn't last long. Eight minutes later, Hibs were back in front. Hearts defender Roddy MacDonald failed to clear a Bobby Thomson header and Willie Irvine steered the ball past Smith. Now it was the Hibs fans turn to gloat with chants of Hibernian FC and hating Jam Tarts and Dundee (Hibees are hard pushed to find anything else to rhyme with FC......) But..........that most celebrated of Hibs players, Ally Brazil, was woefully short with a passback to Rough and Robbo the Boy Wonder raced in to poke the ball into the net to level the scores again. Tynecastle erupted once more. With thirteen minutes to go, Robertson showed another impressive trait when he delivered a glorious twenty five yard cross field pass which carved open the Hibs defence and reached Donald Park. Wee Parky quickly despatched the ball into the penalty box where the old man that was Jimmy Bone headed past Rough to put Hearts in the lead for the first time at 3-2.

Delirium among the home support at Tynecastle. Hibs threw everything at Henry Smith to get the equaliser but Hearts held firm for a famous victory. Maroon shirted players hugged each other and punched the air with delight. It was Hearts first derby victory for almost six years and the first time Hibs had lost in Gorgie for almost a decade. Hearts fans saluted their team at the end of the game and John Robertson had proved he had what it took to perform in the top league. On that day, there was little doubt a star was born.

It was two wins out of two for Hearts and, buoyed by this success, Alex MacDonald's men went on to win their next three league games, including a 3-1 win over Rangers at Tynecastle. Astonishingly, after five games, Hearts were top of the league with maximum points, a remarkable achievement for a side just promoted. Aberdeen then won 2-0 at Tynecastle and the battle for survival commenced but after such a blistering start, Hearts had no serious concerns about relegation. Bone and Robertson were forging an unlikely partnership up front while, in defence, the wise head of Sandy Jardine was an education for Craig Levein who, having signed from Cowdenbeath, was drafted into the Hearts first team earlier than anticipated as a result of injuries. Levein's performances were so impressive, Alex MacDonald found it hard to leave the big Fifer out of the team.

With Motherwell becoming the team this season to become stranded at the bottom of the league – there seemed to be one every year – Hearts won again at Muirton Park on Hogmanay and as Hearts fans toasted the arrival of 1984, they could relax as relegation became only a remote possibility. Indeed, Hearts were looking to finish in the top half of the table and during April they secured draws against the country's four leading clubs – Aberdeen, Dundee United, Rangers and Celtic. That last result – a 1-1 draw against Celtic at Tynecastle – brought remarkable scenes in Gorgie. For, in the words of a popular film at the time – against all odds – Hearts clinched fifth place in the Premier League and a place in the following season's U.E.F.A. Cup. Willie Johnston scored the goal that day and, at 36, it was doubtful if he had ever scored a more important goal in his career. It had been a remarkable season for Hearts. Although knocked out of both cup competitions in the early stages – 7,000 Hearts fans were at Tannadice to see their team lose narrowly to champions Dundee United in the Scottish Cup – it was the league campaign that was the be-all and end-all for the club. Relegation avoided at last. The emergence of some of the best youngsters in the country in the shape of John Robertson, Gary Mackay and Davie Bowman. And European football to look forward to!

When the draw for the first round of the U.E.F.A. Cup was made in July, Hearts fans could scarcely believe the news. Hearts were paired with Paris St. Germain. French football was on a high with the national side having lifted the European Championship in the summer of 1984. Now, Hearts were heading for the same Parc de Princes venue. Having sampled the delights of Douglas Park and Boghead a little over a year before, Hearts fans could hardly wait to head for Paris!

As Hearts supporters pinched themselves in the summer of 1984 just to make sure all this wasn't some kind of dream, Alex MacDonald knew the acid test was about to follow. Having astonished Scottish football, MacDonald knew the pressure would be on Hearts to perform heroics again. And Macdonald, Bone, Jardine and Johnston were a year older – the time to step aside and let younger legs take their place was approaching like an on-coming train. MacDonald signed defenders Brian Whittaker and Kenny Black but, as season 1984-85 got underway, it was evident the team required on-going surgery as results started to go into decline.

In contrast to the previous season, Hearts lost their opening two league games to Dundee United and, worryingly, to Greenock Morton whose match winner that day was a certain Willie Pettigrew. Thanks Willie. What Hearts needed was a game where a win was likely. Just as well then that Hearts headed to Easter Road where Hibs duly obliged by losing 2-1. Forgotten striker Derek O'Connor scored the winner and his celebrations in front of the massed ranks of the Hearts support on the terracing clearly demonstrated that O'Connor's love for Hearts hadn't diminished.

Hearts return to the real big time – European football – came on September 19th when the boys in maroon ran on to the Parc de Princes to face Paris St. Germain. Despite a spirited performance, the gulf in class was obvious. St. Germain were one of the leading sides in Europe whereas Hearts had failed to beat Alloa Athletic less than eighteen months before. The Frenchmen ran out easy 4-0 winners although the chant of Bonjour, Bonjour, Nous Sommes les Gorgie Garcons from the Hearts end in the famous old stadium bemused the residents of the French capital. John Robertson showed how far along the learning curve he had travelled a fortnight later when he scored both Hearts goals in a 2-2 second leg draw – but Hearts were out in the first round on a 6-2 aggregate. It had been a fantastic adventure for everyone and conclusive proof that Hearts were back among the big boys.

However, compared to the previous season, Hearts

were struggling. They lost four league games on the trot and my anxiety was such that I thought Hearts were on the slippery slope back to oblivion. This feeling magnified when, out of the blue, Hearts sold Davie Bowman to Coventry City for £170,000. The old routine eh? Selling our best players at a time when the team was struggling. And I thought Wallace Mercer was different! However, my ignorance in such matters was not an isolated case. Typically, manager Alex MacDonald replaced Bowman for only a fraction of the transfer fee received when he signed Andy Watson from Aberdeen. By now Jimmy Bone was also on his way out and MacDonald persevered with his attempt to sign Sandy Clark from Rangers as a replacement. Initially, Clark refused to head east but the Hearts boss wasn't one for taking no for an answer. Clark was fading out of the first team picture at Ibrox and he eventually signed for Hearts for a modest fee of £30,000. Having slipped perilously close to the relegation trap door, the signing of Sandy Clark was the catalyst to propel Hearts back up the league once more. If Jimmy Bone had been John Robertson's mentor, then Sandy Clark was to prove to be the Head Teacher. Clark scored on his debut in a 3-2 win at Cappielow to exact revenge on Morton's early season win in Gorgie. Wee Robbo also scored that day and another goalden partnership was about to be launched.

Hearts continued to huff and puff throughout season 1984/85 but, thankfully, the newly promoted pair of Greenock Morton and Dumbarton were both finding life at Scotland's top table just a bit too tough. They were both heading for relegation long before the season's end which was just as well from a Hearts point of view although you can always rely on a struggling Hibs team to help you out when all is not well. Sandy Clark endeared himself to those of the maroon persuasion by hitting the winner at Easter Road in the New Years Day derby as Hearts established a stranglehold against Edinburgh's other team. Hearts ended the season in seventh place in the Premier League – one above the Leithers – meaning there was to be no place for the Jambos on the continent in the following season.

Apart from the Paris adventure, what excitement there was in season 84/85 for Hearts came in the cup competitions. Hearts reached the semi-finals of the League Cup where they faced Dundee United. In more than three decades of following Hearts, I can't remember ever seeing them perform well in a cup semi-final. The first leg of this one, at Tynecastle, was a pitiful affair, which United won 2-1. Going to Tannadice would have been difficult enough; going already a goal down would prove nigh on impossible. Typically, Hearts produced their best performance of the season during the first half at Tannadice but, equally typically, lost the game 3-1.

In the Scottish Cup, Hearts defeated Inverness Caledonian 6-0 with a four goal, five star performance from Gary Mackay. They then struggled against First Division Brechin City, requiring a John Robertson goal towards the end at Glebe Park, with its hedge resplendent in all its glory to ensure a replay at Tynecastle which Hearts duly won 1-0. League champions Aberdeen were the quarter final visitors to Tynecastle and a huge crowd of over 23,000 packed into the Gorgie ground on a sunny March afternoon. Hearts were in high spirits for the game. Exactly four weeks previously, Alex MacDonald had taken his side to Pittodrie for a league fixture and had seen Aberdeen race into a two goal lead. But, spurred on by a noisy travelling support in the Beach End, Hearts stormed back with two second half goals – one gleefully scored by Andy Watson against the team who had sold him – and a 2-2 draw was fully merited on the balance of play. The cup-tie at Tynecastle was, well, a typical cup-tie. An enthralling game, end to end with Hearts having the upper hand. From my vantage point in the old enclosure, I was happier with the way the match was progressing than my Aberdeen supporting colleague who was nervously checking his watch. Actions which intensified when Sandy Clark scored through a forest of legs to put Hearts ahead with just twenty minutes left. Hearts supporters sensed a famous victory and the possibility of going all the way to Hampden for the final, especially as Rangers had been knocked out by Dundee in the previous round. But, despite dominating the game, Hearts paid for a moment of hesitancy in defence when Eric Black headed the equaliser towards the end of the game. A midweek replay at Pittodrie was required which was fine for us Hearts fans living in the Granite City, not so for the travelling support. This was another of those nights when Hearts felt an acute sense of injustice both on and off the park. As I paid my way into the Beach End of Pittodrie – the end usually reserved for the away fans – I was astonished to find several hundred Aberdeen fans sitting on the far left hand side with a row of stewards between them and the Hearts support. As the game was pay-at-the-gate, I voiced my concern to one of Grampian Police's finest that there were several hundred Hearts fans still queuing outside and questioned the decision to allow Aberdeen fans in the away end. His response that it was nothing to do with him typified attitudes to football supporters at that time. In the event an estimated 300 Hearts fans had made the 130-mile trip north only to find they were locked out. Because the away end had home fans in it. Hearts subsequent complaints to Aberdeen fell on deaf ears. The club blamed the police, the police blamed the club. It's no 'oor fault didn't pacify those travelling Hearts fans who had a wasted journey.

The game itself was another travesty of justice. Aberdeen, under Alex Ferguson, were ruthless in their pursuit of success and, while they won every domestic trophy and the European Cup Winners Cup under Ferguson's reign, they were not popular winners. When Hearts Roddy Macdonald challenged Eric Black after just fifteen minutes, the Aberdeen forward fell to the ground as if there had been a sniper in the main stand. MacDonald, despite pleading his innocence, was sent off, Aberdeen scored soon afterwards and ten men Hearts Scottish Cup dream was over for another year.

Hearts season collapsed after that and they won just one of their remaining nine league games. The derby match with Hibs at Tynecastle in April was a case in point. Hearts raced into an early two-goal lead through the dynamic duo of Robertson and Clark and another tanking for Hibs looked on the cards. At that time Hibs weren't completely safe from relegation but Hearts contrived to throw away their lead in the final five minutes of the game and it ended 2-2. A crucial point for the wee team – and the Edinburgh derby was safe for another season.....

After the champagne return to the Premier League, season 1984/85 was disappointingly flat. That oft-used cliché 'transitional period' was never more appropriate than this season as Hearts began to phase out the older heads and bring in younger blood. Players such as Brian McNaughton, Malcolm Murray and Jimmy Sandison all got their chance at some stage that season while Stewart McLaren, Donald Park, Jimmy Bone and Willie Johnston bade their farewells.

For the 1985/86 season, manager Alex MacDonald wheeled and dealed in the bargain basement of the transfer market once more. Having failed in an audacious bid to sign Celtic winger Davie Provan, MacDonald instead signed Provan's understudy John Colquhoun in a £50,000 deal while Neil Berry came up north on a free transfer from Bolton Wanderers. Macdonald's aim for Hearts for the season ahead was to qualify for the UE.F.A. Cup once again, having tasted European competition and liked the taste.

Hearts would indeed achieve such a target. But no one was prepared for what was about to happen in the twelve months that followed.......

5

Frank McGarvey Changed My Life
1985-1987

Scottish Cup Final -
an emotional Hearts end

1985-1987

JULY 1985 was memorable for a non-footballing event. Live Aid, the brainwave of Bob Geldof was held at Wembley Stadium, a huge all day concert designed to raise money for the starving millions in Africa. Such events put such matters as football into perspective. That was what I tried to convince myself when Hearts lost match two of season 1985/86 at Love Street to St. Mirren. Well, I say lost. They were annihilated. 6-2 was the final score to the Buddies and Hearts fans could scarcely believe it. Particularly since Hearts had came within seconds of opening the league campaign with a win over Celtic at Tynecastle seven days before. In a fairy tale debut, John Colquhoun put Hearts ahead against his old club only for Paul McStay to hit the equaliser in injury time. But no one prepared us for the Love Street massacre. Hearts had lost 5-2 in Paisley just three months earlier but at least we had the excuse of losing keeper Henry Smith that day due to injury. There was no rhyme or reason for this debacle. Seven days later, Sandy Clark and Walter Kidd were sent off at Ibrox, as Hearts lost 3-1 to Rangers in a match in which the Procurator Fiscal received a report from the police after the sending off incidents got ugly. Well this puts a new slant on things I thought. Hearts already in relegation trouble and with players now in trouble with the law as well.

There was a story at the time, the validity of which was questioned by some people. A Hearts fan was walking on Portobello beach when he found an old lamp. He rubbed it and up popped a genie (as they do) Inevitably, the fellow was told he could have any wish he wanted and it would come true. As he desperately wanted to see his sister in New York but had a phobia about flying, he asked the genie if a bridge could be built over the Atlantic Ocean to enable him to drive over.

'Don't be stupid,' said the genie, 'the logistics involved mean that's an impossibility.'

'Okay, can you fix it for Hearts to win the league championship?'

The genie looked at him. 'Do you want that bridge with two lanes or three?'

I wrote in the last chapter about how you can always rely on Hibs when your team hits a bad spell. Sure enough, Leith's finest came to Tynecastle for a league game having made an even worse start to the league campaign than the JTs. Hibs were rock bottom and remained so after Hearts won 2-1 but the game was an awful one, one of the poorest derby games seen for some time. All you could say was that Hearts were three points clear of their neighbours, but that wasn't saying much. Hearts next opponents both in the league and the league cup were Aberdeen who were in the process of rebuilding Pittodrie Stadium. Yes, quite. Both games were made all ticket with Hearts receiving an allocation of just 400 tickets. This clearly peeved the supporters and angered Wallace Mercer, a man who wasn't slow to make his opinions known to those who cared to listen. They didn't listen in the Granite City so Mercer politely told Aberdeen what they could do with their paltry allocation.

For us Hearts fans who lived in Aberdeen, getting into the game posed little problem – there were plenty seats to be had in the home section and Alex MacDonald's silver shirted men (the away strip used at the time) made it easier for us northern Jambos not to be recognised by refusing to score. Hearts lost the league cup-tie 1-0 and the league game 3-0. When Hearts proceeded to lose games at Motherwell and Clydebank, serious thoughts about relegation entered my head. Okay, Hearts had horrendous injury problems at the time and there were appearances by the likes of Paul Cherry, Brian McNaughton and Colin McAdam, but Hearts fans knew from past experience the folly of losing too many points early in the league campaign. Iain Jardine then hit an equaliser as Hearts scrambled a 1-1 draw against Dundee at Tynecastle on October 5th 1985. A notable date and a notable game as – get this – eight months would pass before Hearts lost again...

On October 12th Hearts faced Celtic at Celtic Park. Hearts record in the east end of Glasgow is woeful to say the least. Sixteen years had elapsed since the JTs had last won there and, given the team's poor start to the season, a win bonus for the players looked unlikely. But this was a significant day. John Robertson scored the only goal of the game (before being stretchered off with what looked at one stage like a broken neck, but later, thankfully, proved to be just bruising) and suddenly, Alex MacDonald's team made people sit up and take notice. Another important win was the single goal victory at Tynecastle over an Aberdeen team who had just defeated a minor team in the league cup final. Hearts now had self-belief in bucketfuls. Rangers and Motherwell were beaten at Tynecastle in the space of seven days and

Hearts were steadily progressing up the Premier League table. The Rangers game was a benchmark on that progress. Hearts coasted to a 3-0 victory and could have won by a greater margin. Then there was one of those curious quirks on which seasons can turn. In October, Scotland secured a 1-1 draw in Wales in a World Cup qualifying game, the aftermath of which saw the tragic death of manager Jock Stein. With the nation in a state of shock, the matter of qualifying for the World Cup in Mexico in 1986 still had to be resolved as the Scots were involved in a play-off game to ascertain their presence at a fourth successive finals. Nothing untoward there you may think – except that Scotland's opponents were.......Australia. Frank McAvennie helped secure a 2-0 win in the first leg at Hampden but Scotland were now faced with a trip to the other side of the world for the second leg in December. Alex Ferguson was in temporary charge of the national side but the Aberdeen manager was not inclined to look to a resurgent Hearts side for any players. So while the likes of Aberdeen, Celtic, Rangers and Dundee United had their league games postponed in order to assist the national side, Hearts were carrying on thank you very much. Clydebank were thrashed 4-1 at Tynecastle on a rather frosty pitch and, just before Christmas, Hearts defeated St. Mirren 1-0 at Love Street. Not only had Alex MacDonald's men avenged the 6-2 drubbing at the beginning of the season, they were now, remarkably, sitting at the top of the Premier Division for the first time in their history. The so-called 'big guns' all had games in hand due to the Scotland situation but, as a popular entertainer with a large chin said at the time, 'points make prizes' and this was the perfect Christmas present for Hearts supporters.

Tynecastle, January 1st 1986. New Years Day had arrived. Hibernian arrived. Close on 30,000 fans arrived, most of them sporting maroon and white and huge grins. Hearts last game had seen them win easily at Ibrox Stadium to more or less eliminate Jock Wallace's Rangers from the championship race. Yes, we were now talking about Hearts challenging for the league title, however bizarre that idea may have seemed a mere four months earlier. The Hearts fans left for the numerous Gorgie hostelries delirious with joy as Hearts skated to a 3-1 win. Happy New Year my Hibernian friends! A fortnight later, Hearts faced the acid test – a trip to Pittodrie to face reigning champions Aberdeen. Alex Ferguson's Dons had not lost at home for over a year and most of the 5,000 Hearts supporters – Pittodrie's new look was now complete – who headed north would have gladly settled for a draw. Indeed a goalless match looked likely when John Colquhoun raced clear of the Aberdeen defence with eight minutes to go and slipped the ball beyond the despairing reach of keeper Jim Leighton. 1-0 to the Gorgie Boys. For a Hearts supporter living in Aberdeen it couldn't get any better than this! Hearts were beginning to open a gap at the top of the league and suddenly the unthinkable was a distinct possibility. Could Hearts actually become league champions?

In the glorious month of March it seemed we could. Hearts won five league games on the bounce, including victories over Hibernian (inevitably) and Rangers (again). Then Hearts secured a truly memorable triumph at Tannadice against a very good Dundee United side. Hearts romped to a 3-0 win and many people thought that, as United were at the time Hearts nearest challengers, the league title was bound for Tynecastle for the first time in twenty-six years. Unbeaten since September, a team full of rejects from other clubs and free transfers was about to create history. Or so we thought. Along with most other Jambos, I was pretty unbearable at that time and would take great pleasure in taunting my Aberdonian associates. Fittingly, Scottish Television decided to screen live the league meeting between Hearts and Aberdeen at Tynecastle on April 20th as the league flag came into sight. The match was moved to the Sunday to accommodate the cameras and it was in this game that the first seeds of doubt were sown in this Hearts fans' mind. Hearts were poor and looked like they were going to suffer a rare defeat when Peter Weir gave Aberdeen the lead from the penalty spot late in the game. But John Colquhoun became the scourge of The Dons yet again when he fired home the equaliser – in the 87th minute......

Hearts held a three point lead at the top of the table and had just two games to play. Dundee United were three points behind – and then lost at home to St. Mirren, ruling Jim McLean's side out of the running to lift the championship for the second time in three years. But, by now, Celtic had crept up, practically unnoticed. Davie Hay's side were four points behind Hearts – but with a game in hand, which they duly won 2-0 at Motherwell. So the final league fixtures of the season saw Hearts need just a single point from their visit to Dens Park to play Dundee while Celtic had to defeat St. Mirren in Paisley by a barrowload of goals while hoping for a Hearts defeat. It was May 3rd – Hearts had been undefeated in all competitions since September 28th.......

That day at Dens Park was one that will never be forgotten by those fans, particularly Hearts fans, who were there. Dundee was an hour and a half away for me and when I got to the City of Discovery at lunchtime the place was heaving with Hearts supporters. Every pub in the city centre was full of expectant Jambos who had travelled to Dundee on an air of celebration. An article in that morning's Daily Record had dragged up the 1965 final day saga when Hearts, needing just a draw at home to Kilmarnock to lift the championship, lost 2-0 – thereby handing the title to the Ayrshire club on goal average. Spurious tabloid mischief making, we declared. But then the rumours began....

At Dens Park as the team warmed up there was no sign of Craig Levein, the most cultured defender in Scottish football. No sign either of full back George Cowie. Wee John Robertson and John Colquhoun were there but they looked like they had been out on the batter all night. Of course they hadn't – they were in the throes of recovery from a sickness bug, which had swept through the squad at the most inopportune time. Levein and Cowie remained in their sick beds. In a throwback to the day when Hearts would struggle to beat the likes of Dumbarton and Alloa Athletic, Walter Kidd and Roddy MacDonald were drafted in to the team. As the game kicked off it was clear this wasn't the same Hearts team that had carried all before them in the preceding eight months. Gary Mackay was struggling in midfield. John Robertson and Sandy Clark were well shackled by the Dundee defence which included a promising youngster called Colin Hendry. Brian Whittaker struggled so badly, he had to be replaced at half-time. An agonising half-time as it turned out because news came through on crackly radios that Celtic were 4-0 up against St. Mirren. In front of me, on the terracing behind the goal, that scoreline nearly instigated a punch up as Hearts fans began to visualise the nightmare scenario. As the game re-started, Dundee dominated. They still had an outside chance of qualifying for the U.E.F.A. Cup and they poured players forward. Hearts were playing poorly and as Dundee won another corner, I glanced at my watch. Eight minutes to go. Eight minutes for Hearts to hang on. Eight, measly minutes....

When the corner kick swung in the ball fell to Dundee substitute Albert Kidd. The former Motherwell man steadied himself before firing the ball into the roof of the net past a despairing Henry Smith. It was Kidd's first goal of the season, in the final game of the season. As the ball hit the back of the net, time stood still for the fifteen thousand Hearts fans who had made the journey to Dens Park. We stood there motionless, as if in a collective bad dream. By now Celtic were 5-0 up. The dream was now a living nightmare. The championship was disappearing fast. Moments later, Kidd doubled his goal tally for the season to make it 2-0 for Dundee and Hearts league title hopes were in tatters.

It was all too much for many Hearts fans, some of whom collapsed to the ground in despair. All I wanted to do was get out of the ground and head back to Aberdeen. My wife was days away from giving birth to our first child but, selfishly, she was furthest from my mind as I trudged back to Dundee Bus Station, head bowed, hoping no one would notice my crumpled maroon and white scarf and ask me what the score was. For only the second time in my life, I cried as the result of a football match. I managed to hold my emotions in check at Dens Park but on the way to the station, I could hold back the tears no more, especially when an old fella on Dens Road realised the situation and offered to shake my hand. My mate walked straight past him as if he weren't there and all I could do was shake my head. The tears began....

It was a long and silent journey back to the Granite City. It had indeed been 1965 all over again although I was too young to remember that first tragedy. But history had repeated itself. Hearts had blown it on the last day of the season. Four years had passed since I saw Hearts lose at home to Motherwell to blow their promotion chances but this was much, much more painful. Smug Aberdonians awaited our arrival back in the pub. I managed one pint and could take no more. I headed home, barely acknowledged the missus and headed straight for bed. Mrs Smith informed me that, with childbirth pending, she felt a bit of pain that day. Think yourself lucky, I replied. My heart has been shorn in two. And with that, symptomatic of what had happened to Hearts championship hopes, I turned off the light.....

There was, however, another matter to attend to before the season finished. No, not the birth of my first child. The Scottish Cup Final. Hearts glorious undefeated run had also seen progress in the Scottish Cup and, yet again, Hearts defeated Rangers at Tynecastle in the third round (3-2 in a memorable game) before Hamilton Academicals, St. Mirren and Dundee United were taken care of. So the final at Hampden beckoned on May 10th 1986 and Hearts cup final opponents were......Aberdeen. Personally, I couldn't have made up such a script. Except that while I had been gloating for months about how my glorious Hearts were going to do the double, glib Aberdeen fans were sniggering about Hearts 'forever blowing doubles' and how there would be more tears from Jambos on cup final day.

The day itself, if not the result, was a memorable one. Hearts boss Alex MacDonald had worried about the fans reaction to the Dundee disaster and whether there would be the same level of support. He needn't have worried. A remarkable turn-out of 40,000 Hearts fans – out-numbering their northern rivals by two to one – gave the team tumultuous backing from start to finish – and beyond. With the emotional scars from seven days earlier still too painful to even begin to heal, Hearts were always going to be the underdogs in the game itself and things weren't helped by the loss of an early John Hewitt goal. The Dons added two more in the second half to run out 3-0 winners and so Hearts astonishing season ended with nothing tangible to show for all their remarkable efforts. Aberdeen duly collected the cup, and they and their fans departed Hampden within minutes of the final whistle. Alex Ferguson's side were so dominant in the 1980s that this latest piece of silverware was just another notch on the trophy room door. Hearts supporters, on the other hand, wanted to savour the atmosphere and stayed long after the final whistle to acclaim their side. A full half an hour after the game had ended, most of the 40,000 maroon and white bedecked fans remained on the Hampden terracings and the public address announcer had to plead with the fans to head home. I headed back to Aberdeen in the company of an Aberdeen fan who had waited patiently in his car for me to arrive. The attendance of more than 62,000 was more than had attended the Celtic v. Dundee United Cup Final twelve months earlier and was a strong indication there was more to Scottish football than the Old Firm.

Three Saturdays in May. The first, Hearts lost the

league championship in Dundee. The second, Hearts lost the Scottish Cup Final at Hampden. The third? My first daughter, Laura, was born, 17th May 1986. By the end of the month I was an emotional wreck!

Hearts tumultuous season was to have an effect on the Scottish game that no one envisaged at the time. In the 1980s, the balance of power in the game had already shifted from the Old Firm in the west to the east of Scotland where Aberdeen and Dundee United – the self-proclaimed New Firm – were dominating the game. Aberdeen had won three league titles, Dundee United one while the Scottish Cup headed for the Granite City four times in five years. The Old Firm, and in particular Rangers, were not happy that the two east coast clubs had passed them by and were determined that Hearts weren't about to do the same. Rangers sacked Jock Wallace early in 1986 and replaced him with an appointment which shook Scottish football – Scottish internationalist Graeme Souness. More importantly, the former Liverpool captain was given a blank chequebook with which to rectify matters and Souness spent millions of pounds to sign the likes of English internationalists Terry Butcher, Chris Woods and Graham Roberts. Celtic would soon follow suit and this penchant for buying success would soon leave clubs like Hearts, Aberdeen and Dundee United trailing behind. But, it was good while it lasted and season 1985/86 will remain forever etched in the memory of those Hearts fans who lived through it.

As Rangers and Celtic began to move ahead, Hearts made the mistake in the summer of 1986 of staying still. Only one new faced was added to the squad which came so close to glory – former England youth cap Wayne Foster, who would go on to write his name in the history books in the years ahead. Hearts started season 1986-87 well enough although a shock defeat by Montrose at Tynecastle in the first round of the League Cup shook us all to the core. I could only stand and stare in disbelief as an old pal of mine from primary school days – Innes MacDonald – swung in the corner that lead to the Gable Endie's second goal. Friends Reunited it was not! Then a run of games that saw just one win in eight was a clear indication that the challenge of last season wasn't about to be repeated. Hearts finished in fifth place, a position that would have been gladly accepted a few years back but, in the context of the previous season, was considered disappointing.

Disappointing isn't quite strong enough a word to describe how Hearts ended their Scottish Cup campaign of 1987. After three games were required to overcome Kilmarnock, nearly 30,000 fans headed for Tynecastle for the visit of Celtic in Round Four. Hearts had won the second replay against the Ayrshire team the previous Monday but concerns about fatigue were evened out by Celtic having also defeated Aberdeen in the Cup on the same evening. A tight, tense game ensued before one of those moments occurred that make following Hearts the rollercoaster it is. Barely fifteen minutes were left when Hearts were awarded a free-kick twenty-five yards from goal. As Celtic frantically tried to organise their defensive wall, wee John Robertson ran up and smacked the ball past an astonished Pat Bonner in the Celtic goal to put Hearts a goal up. Bedlam at Tynecastle! As is their want, the Celts swarmed around the Hearts goal but the JTs held firm and a place in the quarter final was achieved. A sensational result and Hearts were now tipped to go on and lift the trophy, as both members of the Old Firm were now out of the Scottish Cup before the quarter final stage (this was the season Rangers lost in the first round to Hamilton Academicals at Ibrox). Hearts were given another home draw in the next round with Motherwell the visitors and, typically, Alex MacDonald's men struggled to a 1-1 draw. But over 15,000 saw John Colquhoun net the winner in the Fir Park replay and so it was off to Hampden Park again for another semi-final.

By now, I had joined the Granite City Hearts Supporters Club, a fine body of people who undertook the trek to see Hearts home and away every week. It was good company, led by the inimitable figure of Charlie Brown who was as devoted to the boys in maroon as anyone could be. Mind you, the penchant for setting off from Aberdeen at 12.00 noon for Tynecastle took cutting things a bit fine to new levels, particularly as the stop at a Forfar pub for a couple of pints, a pie and a game of pool was considered essential. On the way to Hampden for the semi-final with St. Mirren, the bold Charlie considered it prudent to take the names of those going down to the final. When I ventured that, perhaps it might be worth thinking about this after the game, I was almost kicked off the coach at Dundee – not a place you want to be left stranded. Didn't these fellas know anything about following Hearts? True to form, an injury hit Hearts – without the injured John Robertson – produced their worst performance of the season and lost 2-1, former Celtic striker Frank McGarvey scoring the winner. The trip back to Aberdeen was akin to travelling home from a family funeral. In a fit of pique, I blamed Charlie Brown's arrogance for costing us a return trip to Mount Florida and I ceased my membership with the supporters club with immediate effect. It was yet another game that left

Hearts fans distraught. The chance to lift some silverware had never been better but, once more, the team had blown it when it mattered. I sank into a state of depression that weekend and began to think seriously about where my life was heading. I was unhappy living in Aberdeen, I hated my job which had turned into a nightmare following the Tory government's decision to de-regulate the bus industry and, despite being just 25, I felt nearer 50. After the St. Mirren defeat, I took serious stock of my life and decided on a plan of action that would take me to living in Edinburgh and a new and better life. I gave myself five years to achieve it – and ended up doing it in half that time. So, in many ways, Frank McGarvey changed my life. If the St. Mirren striker hadn't scored the winner in that desperate semi-final, perhaps I wouldn't have thought so deeply about things that weekend. But he did and the agonising result was the trigger for me to transform my unhappy life.

Rangers won the league that season, a remarkable transformation from a team going nowhere to league champions. Well, not too remarkable given the blank chequebook new manager Graeme Souness had been given. The former Liverpool midfield man bought success for Rangers that season and things in Scotland haven't been quite the same since. Either one of the Old Firm has won the championship every season since and it looks increasingly likely that for clubs such as Hearts and Aberdeen, the hope of becoming league champions again is just a pipe dream. Back in 1987 we clung to that dream but as the decade that fashion forgot entered its final stages, things would change both for myself and my family – and my extended family in Gorgie.....

6

One Team in Edinburgh
1987-1994

Fergie sinks the Germans!
Iain Ferguson scores against Bayern Munich,
UEFA Cup quarter final, February 1989

1987-1994

THE PAIN OF THAT SCOTTISH CUP defeat by St. Mirren hurt all through the summer months of 1987. There was no World Cup or European championship to keep fans occupied and, despite Hearts finishing fifth in the Premier League, there was to be no European competition for Jambos to look forward to either. St. Mirren's eventual Scottish Cup triumph – they defeated Dundee United 1-0 in a truly awful final – saw the Paisley Buddies in the European Cup Winners Cup. It was the final knife in the back of a cruel season – had United won, Hearts would have been placed in the U.E.F.A. Cup as the Tannadice men had finished third in the league and were in Europe in any case. But that merely strengthened this writer's view that God had leanings towards a certain team from Easter Road....

Season 1987/88 saw further changes at Tynecastle. Some of these changes astounded the Gorgie faithful given the perilous state of Hearts financial position just five years earlier. Rangers centre half Davie McPherson joined Hearts along with Ibrox full back Hugh Burns for a combined fee of £300,000. This was a clear signal of intent from chairman Wallace Mercer that Hearts weren't content to let Rangers and Celtic race away from them. Manager Alex Macdonald believed the central defensive pairing of McPherson and Craig Levein would be the 'dream ticket' although Levein was still recovering from serious injury sustained the previous October. He returned almost a year to the day of that injury and this meant a retirement from playing for Sandy Jardine who had proved just as invaluable to Hearts as he had done to Rangers in the 1970s. Jardine become the first player to lift the Scottish Footballer of the Year Award twice – his second award coming at the end of that fateful 1985/86 season. Other additions to the Hearts team were Mike Galloway from Halifax Town and Alan Moore from Dumbarton.

Hearts began the season in style. After losing to Celtic and drawing with St. Mirren, Hearts won six league games on the trot which included a highly impressive 5-1 win at Falkirk. Rangers were fortunate to leave Tynecastle with a goalless draw and, remarkably, Alex MacDonald's side were challenging the Old Firm supremacy. But as is always the case with Hearts, just when you think everything in the garden is rosy, calamity strikes. We had become almost blasé when it came to the Edinburgh derby. Since returning to the Premier League in 1983, Hearts had yet to taste defeat against the wee team and the way Hearts had started the season, no one thought it would be any different when a trip to Easter Road beckoned in October. Even John Robertson managed to score his almost customary derby goal that day (who put the ball in the Hibees net? Johnny, Johnny....) but Hibernian produced a rare performance of resilience to record a 2-1 win – their first derby win for almost a decade. That result hurt. I saw it as an omen when Hearts returned my cheque the day before the game telling me the tickets had all been sold, therefore meaning I would miss my first Edinburgh derby since the late 1970s. As signs go, that was rather ominous. They say every cloud has a silver lining and at least I wasn't in Edinburgh to hear the gloatings of those in green and white. Still, one has to be magnanimous...no they don't! Let's just say that Hibs winning the derby doesn't happen very often.

Hearts embarked on an eight game unbeaten run which ended in a thriller at Ibrox where Rangers edged home 3-2. But the JTs were clearly rattling the Old Firm and were in contention for the league title as Christmas approached. After the Rangers loss in November, Hearts went undefeated until the end of February. Then the wheels came off. There was a sequence of only three wins in eleven games including three successive goalless draws. Hearts were left trailing in the championship race although a 6-0 thrashing of St. Mirren at Love Street was almost worth waiting for. Graeme Souness's Rangers capitulated in April leaving Celtic to lift the league flag in their centenary season. As Rangers crumbled, Hearts picked up again and won 2-1 at Ibrox, a result which clinched runners up spot for Hearts in the league. Highly creditable indeed and a testament to Alex MacDonald's ability to get the best out of players deemed not good enough for other clubs. As well as McPherson and Burns, Brian Whittaker, Kenny Black, Sandy Clark and John Colquhoun were all former Old Firm players and Hearts had the label of Old Firm 'rejects'. A label which merely spurred the players to greater heights. However, for the third season in succession, Hearts season was to end in bitter disappointment.

If Alex MacDonald's skill lay in getting the best out of players, the hurdle he found almost impossible to leap was getting his players to perform when it really mattered, on big occasions. For the third season in a row, Hearts progressed to the semi-finals of the Scottish Cup. This time they faced Celtic at Hampden. A Celtic team going for the league and cup double in their centenary season. More than 65,000 packed into Hampden to see a dour game, a typical semi-final – plenty of effort but nae fitba! But with an hour gone Brian Whittaker, of all people, lobbed a speculative cross high into the Celtic penalty box. Keeper Bonnar misjudged it and the ball flew into the net to give Hearts the lead. 25,000 Hearts supporters danced with delight. The defence with Whittaker and McPherson outstanding held firm and with just two minutes to play, Hearts were still ahead. It seemed we were about to lay to rest the ghosts of Hampden past when Celtic were awarded a corner. As the ball swung in, Hearts keeper Henry Smith went to collect – and dropped it. Mark McGhee stroked the ball into the net and Celtic had got out of jail. 1-1 and disconsolate Hearts fans faced up to a midweek replay. Had Hearts chance of a cup upset gone? It sure had – just sixty seconds later. Another corner kick to Celtic. Another dangerous cross. Another attempt by Henry Smith to collect the ball. Another failed attempt. Andy Walker pounced. Another goal for Celtic. 2-1. The referee then blew his whistle for the end of the game. Hearts were out of the Scottish Cup in the most dramatic of circumstances. Jubilant Celtic fans could not contain their glee. Hearts seemed to be taking failure to new heights.

I thought it couldn't get any worse. How many more ways could this team of mine inflict pain and suffering? Surely football was meant to be a joyous thing? All Hearts had given me was abject pain and misery. 1986, 1987 and now this. And the dark clouds of depression deepened when, days later, the news broke that the fans hero, John Robertson, had been sold to Newcastle United for a club record fee of £750,000. Robbo leaving? Surely not? But it was true. The boy who had given so much excitement and pleasure to Hearts fans was on his way. It was the end of Hearts as I knew it. Of the trio of youngsters who had been the club's salvation in the early 1980s, only Gary Mackay was left (Davie Bowman had been sent to Coventry as it were).

For Alex MacDonald the acid test was imminent. Wee Doddie was one of the finest managers around at getting the best out of previously unheralded players. But the sale of John Robertson meant that, for the first time in his managerial career, MacDonald had serious money to spend. Robertson's replacement was Dundee United striker Iain Ferguson – yes, he was also another ex Ranger – and former Hearts favourite Eammon Bannon also left Tannadice to come home as it were. Sadly, Craig Levein suffered another bad injury and was out for months once again. Youngster Alan McLaren was drafted into the team as was Jimmy Sandison.

But Hearts began season 1988/89 poorly, almost as if still hung over from the events of April. The opening eighteen league games brought just two wins. Rumours abounded that all was not well. Hearts were struggling badly for the first time since their return to the top tier of Scottish football in 1983. While the club reached another cup semi-final – this time the League Cup – the subsequent woeful performance in the 3-0 defeat from Rangers at Hampden was the last straw for the Tynecastle board of directors. Chairman Wallace Mercer took action – action which bemused many. He didn't sack Alex MacDonald – he sacked co manager Sandy Jardine. Two pairs of hands on the tiller wasn't working said Mercer.

If things on the domestic front were far from bright, there was a ray of light shining from an unusual source – Europe. For once, the U.E.F.A. Cup draw was kind to Hearts and Irish club St. Patrick's Athletic offered little resistance in the first round as Hearts skated to a 4-0 aggregate victory. When Austria Vienna secured a goalless draw at Tynecastle in the first leg of the second round, it seemed that yet another European campaign would end early. But Hearts produced one of their finest displays in Europe in the return leg in Austria with Mike Galloway heading the only goal to see Hearts head for round three. It was a performance and result which lifted much of the gloom around Tynecastle and there seemed little reason to fear Yuogslavs Velez Mostar. This was confirmed when Hearts romped to a 3-0 win in the first leg at Tynecastle, meaning they could afford a 2-1 defeat in a very hostile return leg. Incredibly, given their poor form at home, Hearts were now in the unchartered waters of the quarter finals of the UE.F.A. Cup. And, inevitably, Hearts drew the plum tie – Bayern Munich.

On the same night that Hearts were creating history in Mostar, chairman Wallace Mercer was delivering the news all Hearts fans wanted to hear. The prodigal son was returning home. Newcastle United had agreed to sell John Robertson back to Hearts for the same fee which they had paid for him six months before. Wee Robbo was back where he belonged. And Hearts had also signed full back Tosh McKinlay from Dundee. A U.E.F.A. Cup quarter final to look forward to. Two new signings including the return home of the legend. No wonder

Hearts defeated Rangers at Tynecastle immediately after the Mostar game!

The visit of Bayern Munich to Gorgie in February 1989 was, naturally, a huge occasion for Hearts. Despite it being a Wednesday night, I made the trip down from Aberdeen and the atmosphere in the Tynecastle shed that night was brilliant. More than 26,000 were inside the ground and the Germans didn't know what hit them! As was Alex Macdonald's way, he simply told his players to get wired in and it was clear the Bundesliga team didn't have the appetite for the more physical side of the game. Midway through the second half with the game still goalless, Hearts were awarded a free-kick outside the Munich penalty box. Tosh McKinlay rolled the ball to Iain Ferguson who let rip with a rasping shot which screamed high into the net. Bedlam at Tynecastle! It was enough to give Hearts a 1-0 lead to take over to Germany and the eyes of the nation turned to the boys in the maroon and white candy striped shirts. Hearts performed admirably in Munich with John Colquhoun hitting the post and coming close to securing the away goal which would have proved crucial. But Bayern did just enough to win 2-0 on the night and go through to the semi-finals 2-1 on aggregate. But Hearts had given one of the best clubs in Europe a helluva run for their money.

Hearts returned from Munich to a Scottish Cup tie at Celtic Park. With emotions high, Alan McLaren and Tosh McKinlay were sent off by the referee for reasons which were beyond most of us sporting maroon. Yet again, controversial refereeing decisions proved costly for Hearts at Celtic Park and Celtic went on to win 2-1. Hearts season had come to a premature end with a sixth place finish in the Premier Division reasonable enough given the way the season had started. And there was still John Robertson's first goal at Tynecastle to savour since his return from Tyneside. It took four months but was well worth the wait. Robbo netted the winner against Hibs with just five minutes to go, after the wee team had taken an early lead. I was unable to get a ticket for the Hearts end but, unsurprisingly, had little difficulty securing a ticket among the Hibs supporters sitting in the old Tynecastle stand. When wee Robbo scored the late winner, I just had to pay a visit to the 'gents'...........!

Alex MacDonald made further additions to the squad for the beginning of season 1989/90. Yugoslav striker Husref Musemic arrived in Edinburgh and was joined by Northern Ireland internationalist David McCreery and midfield player Davie Kirkwood. Hearts made a decent start to the season and Musemic became an instant hero with the fans when he hit the winner against Hibernian at Tynecastle. Big Moose couldn't speak English but he knew how much his goal meant to those of us dancing on the terracings! Personally, I took immense satisfaction – for obvious reasons – from Hearts impressive 3-1 win over Aberdeen at Pittodrie. Chanting to the home fans that this was so friggin' easy didn't happen too often and so I sang it with relish! Young striker Scott Crabbe scored twice that afternoon and there was the emergence of a new nimble strikeforce of John Robertson, John Colquhoun and Crabbe. All small players but all capable of causing havoc. They were certainly scoring plenty of goals and a 6-3 win over Dundee at Tynecastle saw the new 'terrible trio' score five of them. Hearts were well placed in the league without ever looking as if they were going to challenge for the title itself. The New Years Day derby inevitably ended in a 2-0 win for Hearts at

Tynecastle. Hearts domination in Edinburgh was remarkable. This would be another season where Hearts would remain unbeaten against the wee team and while silverware remained elusive to Alex Macdonald and his men, there remained little doubt that there was only one team in Edinburgh.

At the end of 1989, my plan to leave Aberdeen and set up a new life in the capital city had gathered speed. I had several job interviews in Edinburgh but none had proved successful as most prospective employers questioned my motive for leaving Aberdeen. So, in an act of bravado which astounded friends and family alike, I packed in my job in the Granite City – it had been affecting my health in any case – sold our house and moved in with my father in Paisley with the intention of moving to Edinburgh. As my wife had given birth to our second daughter just three months before and our first daughter was just three and a half years old, most associates had assumed I had gone off my trolley. But the plan worked. Within three months of leaving Aberdeen, I had secured a job and moved the family into rented accommodation in Gorgie. In a flat overlooking the open terraces of Tynecastle! Things couldn't have worked out any better!!

The timing of me getting a job in Edinburgh was crucial. Crucial because the Saturday before the interview, Hearts were at Pittodrie for a Scottish Cup quarter final with Aberdeen (yes, the irony wasn't lost on me) With Hearts league form impressive and the new, nippy front three of Crabbe, Robertson and Colquhoun scoring for fun (copyright Ron Atkinson), many were tipping Hearts to go all the way to the Scottish Cup Final. Some were even thinking Hearts were set at last to break the trophyless hoodoo and get some reward for their years of suffering and hard luck stories. A 1-1 draw at Celtic Park in the league just a week before meant the bookies made Hearts as favourites to defeat the Dons. But we all know what happens when Hearts are expected to do something and are close to success. The roof caves in. And the metaphoric roof at Pittodrie crashed in on Hearts that day as Aberdeen won 4-1. Another year, another dream in tatters. Five thousand Hearts supporters had made the long journey north that day and, for the first time that I had been aware of, murmurings of discontent were being heard about the manager. Just how many near things could Hearts fans stomach? Why did the team's bottle always go when it mattered most? Was it Alex MacDonald's fault?

Hearts ended the season in joint second place with Aberdeen with Rangers cruising to the league championship once again (Celtic had plummeted to fifth place just ten points above relegated Dundee). The 1990s would see many more changes at Tynecastle, the first of which was just a matter of weeks away.

Hearts at least showed signs of ambition by signing Rangers midfield player Derek Ferguson for £750,000. Ferguson was a stylish player who, nonetheless, didn't quite fit in with the Souness revolution at Ibrox. It was seen as a major coup for Hearts to sign someone of his undoubted ability. Season 1990/91 began with a home game against St. Mirren. Having kicked off the two preceding seasons with defeats from Celtic, Hearts fans looked for a winning start to the first league campaign of the new decade. The game ended 1-1. Defeat followed the following week at Dunfermline and from looking at topping the league after the first couple of games, Hearts were instead languishing near the bottom. A midweek trip to Aberdeen for a League Cup tie wasn't the most enticing of fixtures. The game was broadcast live by fledgling satellite television company BSB and only a few hundred die-hard Jambos made the trip north. Having spent several years in the Granite City and having finally achieved my ambition of beginning a new life in Edinburgh, my wife found it difficult to accept that I was breaking a family holiday from the silver sands of Lossiemouth to head for Aberdeen on a dreich Wednesday night. Of course Hearts didn't appreciate my efforts and lost 3-0. The murmurs of discontent among the supporters became more amplified, particularly as big signing Derek Ferguson started the game as a substitute. With Hearts two goals down at half-time, manager Alex MacDonald did indeed make a change at half-time – he brought on Walter Kidd. For the first time there were chants of MacDonald Must Go from disenchanted Hearts supporters.

Three days later, Rangers came to Tynecastle and won rather more easily than the 3-1 scoreline suggested. Wallace Mercer had already shown he wasn't afraid to make tough decisions. Two days after the Rangers defeat, Alex MacDonald was sacked. Although Hearts were struggling, the decision to remove the man who taken the club back to the top table of Scottish football and who so nearly achieved an incredible league and cup double four years earlier shook Scottish football. The players were stunned, some of them – notably Gary Mackay and John Robertson – were in tears. Some supporters were also upset and vented their anger on Wallace Mercer. It had already been a difficult summer for the chairman who astounded the football world in June when he announced his intention to buy Hibernian and merge them with

Hearts to create a 'super club' in Edinburgh. Supporters of both Hibs and Hearts soon made it clear where Mercer could stick his plans for such a venture. Now Mercer was targeted again although many Hearts supporters were of the view that a change had to be made. I felt MacDonald had lost his way, perhaps he had been in charge of the team for too long. Big money was now a factor in Scottish football and it was clear that MacDonald was uncomfortable with spending hundreds of thousands of pounds for one player. He was much happier picking up players for next to nothing and making them feel an important part of his team. Alex MacDonald left Tynecastle in September 1990 with his dignity and professionalism intact. It was typical of the man that he personally thanked every Hearts player for their efforts before he left Gorgie for the last time. He had gone but he would never be forgotten.

Wallace Mercer was probably thinking of what Graeme Souness had done at Rangers when considering MacDonald's replacement. Souness was a former Scottish internationalist who had played at the top level in England and Italy. Joe Jordan was from the same stable, having played for Scotland in three World Cups and having tasted success with Leeds United, Manchester United and AC Milan. Jordan had turned down the chance to manage Aston Villa a few weeks earlier so one doubted whether the man with the famous gap tooth grin would accept Mercer's invitation to come to Tynecastle. But one learned that it was always unwise to doubt Wallace Mercer and Joe Jordan was duly installed as Hearts manager at a packed press conference. Once again, Mercer had pulled off a coup.

1990/91 was to be a strange kind of season. Changing

the manager only three games in was bound to have an unsettling effect and there were those who wanted Sandy Clark, who was by now a coach, to be given the manager's job – particularly as he had been in temporary charge and had led Hearts to a 3-0 win over Hibernian at Easter Road. It may appear to any non Hearts fan reading this book that Hearts have enjoyed consistent success against their city neighbours. Well, the facts don't lie. On Jordan's appointment, however, Hearts lost to St. Johnstone, St.Mirren and Aberdeen as well as a heavy loss at Ibrox. In between those games was a 1-0 win over Celtic. You get the picture. The New Year Derby was at Easter Road and, yes, Hearts won it. In fact it was arguably the maroon's best performance of the season and the 4-1 victory could and should have been greater. The four goals were scored by the unlikely foursome of Tosh McKinley, Dave McPherson, Craig Levein and Gary Mackay. John Robertson may well have had an off day – just as well for the Hibees!

From the sublime to the ridiculous and Hearts lost 5-0 at Pittodrie a month later. Hearts finished fifth in the league, well adrift of the top four. The league was to be expanded to twelve clubs the following season which was just as well for Hibernian as they would have been relegated to the First Division. Hearts season was summed up when they fell at the first hurdle in the Scottish Cup – to First Division Airdrieonians at Broomfield. In addition there was another typical Hearts scenario in the U.E.F.A. Cup. I had planned to travel with Hearts on their European travels that season and eagerly anticipated the First Round draw. It was with bated breath that I heard the name of our opponents – Dnepr Dnepropetrovsk. Well, thank you U.E.F.A. I didn't fancy a trip to a Soviet Union that was in the throes of breaking up, particularly as Dnepr played about forty miles away from the location of the Chernobyl nuclear explosion of 1986. Hearts performed admirably, securing a tremendous 1-1 draw in the first leg away before finishing the job 3-1 in the return leg at Tynecastle. Italian side Bologna were next up and in the first leg at Tynecastle, Hearts played some magnificent football in the first half and were 3-0 up at half-time. But you know the script, don't you? Goalie Henry Smith was deemed to be time wasting early in the second half and a free-kick was subsequently awarded to Bologna. The Italians scored, the game ended 3-1 to Hearts and our beloved team crashed 3-0 in the return leg in Italy to go out 4-3 on aggregate. Given what happened in that first forty five minutes at Tynecastle, it was quite unbelievable that Hearts should lose the tie. But you'll often find the words unbelievable and Hearts in the same sentence.

So Hearts fans waited for the Jordan effect to materialise in season 1991/92. Jordan's knowledge of the game south of the border saw players such as Graeme Hogg, Glyn Snodin and Steve Penney arrive at Tynecastle as well as a striker who gave Hearts a physical presence in the penalty box – Ian Baird. Hearts got off to a highly impressive start to the season by winning their first four games and not tasting defeat until game number ten – and that was at Celtic Park. But despite a forward line of Baird, Robertson and Crabbe, the goals weren't exactly flowing and it looked like the results were the be all and end all rather than the performances for Joe Jordan. But no one could argue with the results. Hearts won nine out of ten matches during November and December and hit the top of the Premier Division. On January 4th 1992,

Hearts won 2-1 at Celtic Park and it looked like Joe Jordan was about to lead Hearts into a serious championship challenge for the first time in six years. A week later, Aberdeen came to Tynecastle – and, inspired by a wonder performance by youngster Eoin Jess, romped to a 4-0 win. Hearts confidence was shot to pieces. A week later they lost to Airdrieonians and then to Rangers. Hopes of a league title vanished. Hearts did finish runners up to Rangers though, albeit nine points behind (in the days when only two points were awarded for a win) The Scottish Cup brought inevitable disappointment, once again at the semi-final stage. And once again it was a semi-final Hearts were expected to win given that Airdrieonians were the opponents. But a woeful goalless draw was followed by an equally woeful replay in which Hearts lost in a penalty shoot-out. Would Hearts ever win at Hampden?

Despite yet more pain at the national stadium, there was hope (there's always hope!) that Hearts would progress under Joe Jordan. Season 1992/93 would see Jordan have a full season in charge (or so we thought) but the problem – as ever – was the lack of money he would get to seriously strengthen the team. The Old Firm were spending cash like there was no tomorrow and while Hearts could never compete with some of the Glasgow duo's outrageous transfer fees, the manager was left to deal in the bargain basement of available players – a sort of What Other Managers Do Not Want. For the new season, Peter Van de Ven moved to Gorgie from Aberdeen while former Motherwell midfielder Ally Mauchlen, who had went to Leicester City along with Gary McAllister a decade earlier, signed a short-term deal. Forced to wheel and deal, manager Jordan tried to sell Scott Crabbe to Dundee United. Crabbe, a died-in-the-wool Jambo, promptly threw a spanner in the works by saying he didn't want to play for anyone else other than his beloved Hearts. Some managers would be delighted with such a show of loyalty but Jordan was angered and dropped the striker. Dundee United, sensing all was not well, were persistent and eventually Crabbe agreed to head north when it became clear he had no future at Tynecasle under Joe Jordan. It was a messy saga and the Hearts fans weren't exactly appeased when Tannadice reserve player Allan Preston came to Gorgie as part of the deal – and immediately found himself in the first team.

Hearts were grinding out results without playing particularly attractive football. A 6-2 hammering by Aberdeen at Pittodrie was too much for me personally (I left Pittodrie when the fifth goal went in) and it began a sequence of results which included defeats to Falkirk and Airdrieonians and a draw with St. Johnstone. The natives were restless. Hearts weren't making progress – in fact they were going back the way. A goalless draw with the wee team in the New Year Derby at Easter Road seemed to typify Hearts season – much ado about nothing. Struggling in mid table the team seemed unable to cope with the rigours of a forty four game league season. By April it was evident the players were unhappy as well. Hearts lost to Rangers, Motherwell and Aberdeen before heading for Brockville to face a soon to be relegated Falkirk. The players seemed to be clueless to what system the manager wanted them to play. Falkirk were 2-0 up at half-time, scored a couple of early second half goals and the players seemed to 'down tools'. Hearts ended up losing 6-0. I, and several other Hearts fans, stormed out of the crumbling old ground when the fifth goal went in shortly after five past four. I vowed never to go back to watch Hearts again. I was supping a pint in Ryries Bar in the Haymarket at the time the referee blew his whistle for the end of the game. 'Bitter?' asked the woman behind the bar. 'No – just very angry' I replied.

I wasn't the only one. Wallace Mercer called Joe Jordan into his office the following Monday and told the manager he was on his way. The big gamble had not paid off. Hearts season had ended with a Scottish Cup semi-final defeat – stop me if you've heard this before – to Rangers at Celtic Park. Ironically, the match winner was Davie McPherson who had been transferred back to Rangers the summer before. After that 2-1 defeat, the Hearts players seemed to have a not so hidden agenda – to get rid of a manager whose tactics they neither approved nor understood.

Sandy Clark was back in charge of the team until the end of the season. Having led the Hearts under 18s to Youth Cup success, Clark introduced some of them to the first team as there was nothing to lose for the final few games of the season. Allan Johnston, Gary Locke and Tommy Harrison at least gave Hearts fans some hope for the future.

At the end of season 1992-93, by God, we needed something.

7

It's Hearts, Jim.........
1993-1996

Hearts legend Gary Mackay

1993-1996

AT THE BEGINNING OF SEASON 1993/94 Sandy Clark was given the manager's job at Tynecastle on a permanent basis – okay, I won't define the word permanent – and with the former Jambos striker's penchant for giving youth its fling, it was a move that went down well with most Hearts fans. The aforementioned Johnston and Locke as well as Kevin Thomas were to become regulars in the Hearts team this season. Allan Johnston, in particular, was a throwback to the old fashioned wingers of the 1950s and 1960s and when he got the ball the anticipation level rose among the Hearts support. But Clark knew that putting too many youngsters in the team at once was tantamount to disaster and he brought in a couple of, shall we say, more experienced players.

In the Hearts line up for the opening league game of the season – at Ibrox – was striker Justin Fashanu. 'Fash' once scored the BBC Television goal of the season whilst playing for Norwich City and had been transferred to Nottingham Forest for £1 million several contracts ago. In 1993 he was, as they say, in the twilight of his career and had joined Airdrieonians the previous season. Sandy Clark clearly saw something to persuade the striker to come to Tynecastle. Just what, we weren't exactly sure. Fash scored just one goal and his final appearance in the first team was in October. It was alleged that, during a particularly woeful game, Clark bawled to Fashanu that

99

he was getting pulled off at half time. There was no truth in the rumour that Fash's response was 'great, at Norwich all we got was an orange........'

Fashanu's private life attracted more publicity than his exploits on the football field and it was clear the Hearts board of directors sat uneasily in the boardroom as they pored over the newspapers. Fashanu was soon on his way and he was to die at a tragically young age a few years later.

Sandy Clark clearly wanted a big name to play up front and, after Fashanu, there came another signing which attracted the media to Tynecastle like Hearts fans to the Diggers for a pint after a game – Maurice Johnston. Johnston was, of course, the first high profile Catholic to play for Rangers, having already told Celtic he was going to return to Celtic Park in 1989. Five years later, Johnston was playing for Everton and Sandy Clark saw Mo as the man who could score goals for Hearts as well as add a few hundred to the gate. We all waited for Maurice to pose with a maroon and white scarf and declare that Hearts were the only club he would come back to Scotland for but, to his credit, the former Scotland striker gave us none of that rubbish, merely saying he was grateful for the opportunity of first team football. Johnston's league debut for Hearts came at Easter Road – probably no better place to be if you want to begin your Hearts career on a winning note. Hearts won 2-0 although it was a Tynecastle legend – John Robertson – who put the ball in the Hibees net. Twice.

But season 1993/94 was to prove a miserable season for Hearts. It's a curiosity that Hearts league form often seems to struggle when the club are involved in European competition. Hearts fifth place finish the previous season, despite Joe Jordan's departure, was enough for U.E.F.A. Cup qualification. And, yet again, Hearts were given a tough first round draw. Atletico Madrid may be the poor relations of the Spanish capital and when Hearts beat them 2-1 in the first leg at Tynecastle, those of us heading to Madrid for the second leg were quietly confident of Sandy Clark's men causing an upset. Our preparations for the second leg were somewhat frazzled. After watching Hearts defeat Celtic in a league game at Tynecastle, we fell on to the coach parked outside the ground three hours later to take us to the continent. 36 hours later we fell off the coach in Madrid on a warm, Monday morning, some of us more than the worse for wear. If I was to write about even some of the exploits of Jambos on that trip, then this book would have to be moved to the top shelf of any half decent book shop so I'll spare you the gory details. Suffice to say we learned the lingo – dos beros, por favor – and we survived (despite our coach driver almost dropping us off at the home end of the Vincent Caulderon stadium – gave a new meaning to the term Spanish fly...) Which is more than the team did as Atletico cruised to a 3-0 win. Their third goal – the one that finally killed Hearts hopes – slipped through the fingers of keeper Henry Smith. Now where have we heard that before? Of course we had been sampling Spanish hospitality all day and were still singing inside the ground half an hour after the end of the game, much to the bemusement of the locals. Most of the players duly came back on to the pitch to applaud the superb travelling support. It was only when Chairman Wallace Mercer emerged, no doubt expecting a similar accolade, that we turned our backs and headed back to the hotel.....

After victory at Easter Road, the JTs went twelve

games without a win and were again struggling against relegation. The Scottish League had decided a twelve club Premier Division with forty-four games just wasn't working and the 'elite' league was to revert back to ten clubs. This meant three clubs would go down this season. Hearts managed to draw with both Celtic and Rangers twice but their form against the other clubs was abysmal. Even Hibs managed a draw at Tynecastle in the New Year derby. Hearts went six games without a win during April, not the month to have a dip in form (not that Hearts form was at any great heights in any case). There were two games left – Dundee United at Tynecastle and Partick Thistle at Firhill. Sandy Clark's men needed to win both to avoid the drop. Nearly 14,000 turned up to a Tynecastle beginning to look like a building site (the ground was in the first throes of redevelopment) for the Dundee United game. The travelling United fans were shepherded into the upper section of the old stand while the Gorgie Road end was opened up to the home support. I went there for the first time in years and the unusualness of the day merely added to my discomfort. An extremely tense game ended with Craig Levein and Stevie Frail – known as Shaggy to one and all – scoring to give Hearts a priceless 2-0 victory. Levein has served Hearts well both as player and Head Coach but it's debatable if he ever scored a more important goal for the club than that one. Results elsewhere meant that Hearts could afford a draw at Firhill the following week. Nonetheless, five thousand Hearts fans headed west to support the team and they were rewarded when Alan McLaren scored the only goal of the game. It had been a close call but Hearts had survived.

It had been a long, arduous slog in the league and the

League Cup had proved short and not sweet, Falkirk defeating Hearts in the second round at Tynecastle. The Scottish Cup, though, brought a game that is still talked about today. After Maurice Johnston scored the only goal to knock out Partick Thistle at Firhill, our joy on the way back to Glasgow Queen Street station intensified when we discovered our opponents for the next round – Hibernian at Easter Road. Thank you very much, the S.F.A. The game was moved to a Sunday to allow the B.B.C. to show it live on television. That didn't stop 21,000 fans heading for Easter Road and a game for the history books. Hearts had last played a Scottish Cup tie there in 1979 when crowd trouble marred Hibs 2-1 quarter final win. Almost fifteen years later, a typically tight, tense game was tied at 1-1 with just five minutes to go. Suddenly, Gary Mackay played one of those through balls, which he did so well and a Hearts striker was through, one on one with goalkeeper Jim Leighton. But the striker wasn't Maurice Johnston or John Robertson. It was substitute Wayne Foster. Now Fozzy had pace, commitment and courage. But he wasn't the world's greatest finisher. I'd lost count of the number of times Fozzy raced down the wing, outpacing the opposing defence only to scuff his cross into the crowd. Similarly, when presented with a chance in the penalty box, the odds on Fozzy ballooning the ball into the terracing were considerably shorter than those of John Robertson. Our joy at a genuine chance for Hearts to win the game was tempered when we realised it was Wayne Foster who was haring in on goal. As Hibs keeper Leighton raced to the edge of his penalty box to meet him, Fozzy struck the ball. The ball whizzed through Leighton's spindly legs and you could hear the net whish as the ball nestled in the goal.

For a split second, 10,000 Hearts fans stood open-mouthed. Then – delirium! By George, Fozzy had done it! Fozzy had scored!! Unbridled joy as the massive Hearts support danced on the steep, crumbling Easter Road terracings. I put the nanosecond pause in celebrations down to most of the 10,000 Jambos scouring the terracing to see where Fozzy had placed his shot. But, the former England youth cap – yes, Fozzy had played in the same England youth team as Gary Lineker – had scored the winner and Hearts were through to the quarter finals. Hibs were out. Even Derek Johnstone, the former Rangers striker now doing his television pundit routine for the BBC, gave the thumbs up from the perilously situated television gantry in the Hearts end. Inevitably, Hearts lost 2-0 to Rangers at Ibrox in the quarter final. But you can still hear the Hearts fans chant at derby games to this day – 'Wayne, Wayne, Super Wayne!'

As the song goes, the times, they were a changing. The Taylor Report, brought in by the Government following the Hillsborough disaster at Sheffield in 1989, decreed that top flight clubs in England and Scotland required to have all-seated stadia. Despite the odd piece of cosmetic work, nothing substantial had been done to Tynecastle for three decades but the days of standing on the terracings were coming to and end. Supporters were asked to raise money to help redevelop Tynecastle. Wallace Mercer had already spent a considerable sum of money on a feasibility study in order that Hearts could move to a new stadium on the outskirts of Edinburgh. The cost and the political unwillingness of the city fathers to destroy green belt areas of the capital meant Hearts had no real choice but to stay put in Gorgie. The bulldozers moved in during the spring of 1994 and the old shed was the first relic to go. The Wheatfield Stand would be the first development, a stand holding 6,000 seats. In time, Tynecastle would become one of the best stadia in Scotland but seeing it reduced to little more than rubble in 1994 brought a lump to the throat of this dewy-eyed Hearts fan.

The wind of change at Tynecastle soon blew into hurricane proportions. Wallace Mercer sold his majority share holding in Hearts to catering supremo Chris Robinson and Edinburgh solicitor Leslie Deans, both life-long Hearts supporters. This was truly the end of an era. Mercer had saved Hearts from certain bankruptcy in 1981 and while he wasn't flavour of the month with every Hearts fan, it's worth considering where Hearts would be today if it hadn't been for the property tycoon. Chris Robinson had his own ideas of how to lead Hearts and one of the first things he did on taking over as Chief Executive was to dismiss Sandy Clark. True, Hearts had struggled since Clark took over as manager but many supporters thought such a decision was unjust. The ramifications of such a move would be felt several years later although not in the way anyone imagined at the time.

A few days before Clark's dismissal, Motherwell manager Tommy McLean suddenly left the Fir Park club in a move, which astounded nearly everyone. McLean had guided Motherwell to a famous Scottish Cup win in 1991 and it was generally thought he had a job for life in Lanarkshire. The reason for his decision became apparent a few days later. Chris Robinson unveiled McLean as the new Hearts manager. A new-look Tynecastle. A new chairman. A new manager. But I didn't feel like dancing along the streets of Gorgie. The new set-up sat uneasily with most Hearts fans. It was unusual for Hearts to appoint a manager who had no previous connection whatsoever with the club. Bobby Moncur had been the last and he lasted less than twelve months. A telltale sign if ever there was one....

Tommy McLean's tenure at Tynecastle was short and not so sweet. McLean had a very clever football brain and his tactical knowledge was second to none. But, it's fair to say he had a negative aura about him with the players seemingly far from sure of what he wanted them to do. Mclean's brief spell couldn't have got off to a worse start – and the season hadn't even begun! Hearts played Raith Rovers in a pre-season friendly at Starks Park. Team mates Craig Levein and Graeme Hogg displayed a will to win by getting involved in a heated argument during the game and punching each other's lights out. Both were sent off the field and the incident was caught on video. An embarrassment of huge proportions to the club and McLean – a strict disciplinarian – was apoplectic. Hogg was to make just one more appearance for Hearts – and that as a substitute – but it wasn't just the Aberdonian and the Fifer who were unhappy.

Hearts began season 1994/95 with just one point from their opening four games. Alarmingly, one of those defeats came when Hibernian bucked a trend by recording a rare win at Tynecastle. Another long battle against relegation beckoned. The fans were unhappy and not slow to voice their dissatisfaction. However, McLean steadied the ship by bringing in former Aberdeen and Rangers player Jim Bett and his influence in midfield calmed the nerves. Hearts defeated Partick Thistle, Celtic and Aberdeen and headed for Easter Road in a better frame of mind. But despite a goal from John Robertson,

Hearts lost their second Edinburgh derby on the trot and there was angst on the terracings. It would be Boxing Day until Hearts won again. Was this what Alex MacDonald had been sacrificed for four years previously? Apart from one season, Hearts had struggled since.

Tommy McLean brought in players such as Colin Cramb, Craig Nelson, David Hagen and Colin Miller as well as Bett. And he showed he wasn't worried about winning any popularity contests with the supporters by signing former Hibs players Brian Hamilton and Willie Jamieson. The signing of Hamilton, in particular, perplexed many Jambos as the player wasn't popular at Easter Road and Hibees gloated at the news he was on his way across the capital. As the season entered its closing phase, Hearts recorded what proved to be two crucial victories. Champions Rangers were beaten 2-1 at Tynecastle whilst a David Hagen goal gave Hearts victory over Celtic at Hampden (Celtic's temporary home while Celtic Park was redeveloped). But Hearts lost again at Easter Road and the final game of an anguished season came at Tynecastle against Motherwell. Hearts had to win to avoid the dreaded relegation play-off against First Division champions Dunfermline Athletic. Ironically, it was the much-maligned Brian Hamilton who gave Hearts the lead and a John Robertson penalty secured a crucial victory. Relief was palpable at Tynecastle. Bizarrely, Hearts results against the Old Firm were impressive and Tommy McLean's team were undefeated by Celtic all season, while memorably knocking Rangers out of the Scottish Cup on a freezing Monday night at Tynecastle (the fixture was changed for live television coverage – again) Hearts were 2-0 up at half-time, dragged back to 2-2 before John Robertson and Kevin Thomas scored late goals for a remarkable 4-2 win. Robertson later remarked that after the game, the manager had torn strips off them for throwing away a two goal lead. Four goals against the league champions to knock them out the cup and still Tommy McLean was an angry man! He must have been seething when Hearts made it to the semi-finals. Can you guess what happened? A Scottish Cup semi-final at Hampden? Against, er, Airdrieonians? Yep. Hearts lost 1-0. And the Airdrieonians manager? Alex MacDonald....

As a former Hearts manager led out an unfashionable team in the Scottish Cup Final at Hampden, Hearts supporters reflected ruefully. The club seemed on another downward spiral, similar to that endured in the 1970s and we all knew where that led. Wee Tommy McLean's ideas about how the game should be played were clearly different to those of the fans. Even the youngsters like Allan Johnston, Tommy Harrison and Gary Locke found their first team chances increasingly limited while unheralded players such as Colin Cramb were making the starting eleven. A perfect example of the manager's way of thinking came in the League Cup exit at home to First Division St. Johnstone. Hearts were two goals up before having Shaggy Frail sent off. Morale was such that the team crumbled and the Perth Saints stormed back to win 4-2. Young Tommy Harrison was brought on as a substitute in the second half – only for McLean to haul the lad back off again after fifteen minutes. Little wonder Harrison never made a name for himself at Tynecastle.

Behind the scenes it was obvious Chris Robinson and his board of directors shared the concerns of the supporters. Tommy McLean left Tynecastle in May 1995 and the club was looking for its fifth manager in as many years. McLean's departure though had the effect of lifting the pall of gloom that hung heavily over Tynecastle. Chris Robinson, meantime, had his eye on a successor. Falkirk had beaten Hearts three times in the Premier League in the season that had just ended and, indeed, the Bairns had finished in fifth place in the final league table, their highest ever position in the Premier League. Their manager was a man not unknown to us long sufferers in Gorgie. Jim Jefferies was a centre half of the 1970s Hearts team that yo-yoed between the Premier and First Divisions and his final year as a Hearts player was in 1981. Jefferies finished his playing days at Berwick Rangers before coaching his local side in Lauder in the borders. Jefferies returned to Berwick as manager and it was obvious that Jefferies the manager was going to be more of a success than Jefferies the player. He built an attractive team at Shieffield Park and when Falkirk called on his services it was another step up the managerial ladder. Jefferies not only got Falkirk promotion to the Premier Division he got them playing an attacking, attractive style of football as those of us who witnessed the 6-0 thrashing of Hearts in 1993 knew only too well. Jefferies reputation blossomed when his Falkirk team went to Ibrox and knocked Rangers out of the League Cup in 1994. With his Tynecastle history, he was the only real choice for Chris Robinson and the board.

Yet, Jefferies declined Hearts initial offer. Standing outside the crumbling edifice that was Brockville, JJ told the media scrum that he was staying put. Falkirk chairman George Fulston was delighted and said that was that. But Chris Robinson isn't a man who gives up easily. Sensing Jefferies unease at turning the Hearts job down, the Chief Executive got back in touch with the man who had transformed Falkirk. Jim Jefferies, grateful to be given a second chance, changed his mind and headed for a Tynecastle that was slowly taking shape with the Wheatfield Stand and Roseburn Stands now complete.

Falkirk were understandably furious. Things weren't helped by the fixture list for season 1995/96, which saw Falkirk at Tynecastle in only the second week of the season. A large travelling support vented their anger at Jefferies that day but the new Hearts boss felt vindicated as his new charges won 4-1 with a display of attacking football, which seemed an alien concept to Hearts fans fed a diet of negativity under Tommy McLean. Hearts used a huge amount of players during the season as Jim Jefferies rebuilt the team whilst still trying to achieve results on the park. Jefferies brought in players such as Alan Lawrence, Neil Pointon, Pasquele Bruno and Hans Eskilsson. Before a midweek league cup tie at home to Dunfermline Athletic, the grapevine was buzzing with the news that Hearts had made a big name signing and he was going to make his debut that evening. When Tynecastle p.a. Mark McKenzie announced in his inimitable fashion 'and making his Tynecastle debut' we all held our breath. 'Let's hear it for David Winnie'. Never has a Tynecastle signing been greeted with such apathy! Winnie gave his all but he was not exactly one of Jefferies more inspired signings and was on his way within two months. Hearts won that night but it was the quarter final tie at Dens Park against First Division Dundee that brought it home to the new manager just how much work was required. The tie ended 4-4 with Hearts, inevitably, losing on penalty kicks. Bad enough except that Hearts losing penalty was taken by goalkeeper Henry Smith as the rest of the team fudged responsibility. Oor Henry was never fazed by such matters – and promptly blazed his penalty over the bar and out of Dens Park. In all probability, the ball may well be bobbing about the River Tay to this day. What was striking that night – if you'll pardon the pun – was that eight of the team had played in the fateful 1985/86 season. Almost a decade before – Jefferies knew things had to change.

The new manager wasn't afraid to give youth its chance and he threw young Paul Ritchie into the team for his debut – against Celtic at Tynecastle. But there were, perhaps, too many changes too soon. When Hearts travelled to Brockville to face a still bitter Falkirk side at the end of October, they had won just two league games. A 2-0 defeat at Jefferies former employers capped a miserable day for all Jambos. Gloating Falkirk fans rubbed in the fact that Hearts had now fallen to the bottom the league. 'You and Judas deserve each other' a Falkirk fan bawled at me as I waited for the train at Grahamston Station. Just as well my missus wasn't with me or she may have got the wrong idea...

Jefferies brought in a new goalkeeper that day – Frenchman Gilles Rousset. He joined Eskilsson and Bruno as the new 'foreign legion' in Gorgie and the affable goalkeeper was to prove a great favourite among the fans. Rousset had played once for the French national side – at Wembley against England and Alan Shearer – and the more cynical among us wondered if the goalie, who would often declare his amour pour les jambos, had perhaps broken a mirror since gaining his one and only international cap. From France at Wembley to Hearts at Brockville in three short years! Nonetheless, the presence of Rousset and Bruno helped to steady the Hearts defensive ship and gave confidence to the younger lads such as Ritchie and Gary Locke. Team spirit had improved dramatically since the previous season and Hearts slowly began to climb the league table.

1996 began with defeat at Easter Road although Neil Pointon did his popularity with the Hearts support no harm at all by joyously celebrating his first goal for the club. Given Hearts tendency to blow hot and cold, it was only a matter of time before the former Everton player was given the nickname 'Disa'...(yeah, I know) But then Partick Thistle, Motherwell and Falkirk were all defeated as Hearts headed for mid table respectability – and a remarkable game at Ibrox on January 20th. Rangers were league champions, sat top of the table and seemingly coasting to yet another league title. Hearts, however, produced one of the biggest shock results in living memory. Allan Johnston, despite his boyhood affection for Rangers, turned in an inspired performance that day and hit a memorable hat-trick – the first opposing player to achieve such a feat at Rangers ground since Alex Ferguson in the 1960s. Hearts won 3-0 and could – and indeed should – have had more that day as Jim Jefferies tactics worked perfectly. Content to sit and absorb Rangers pressure, Hearts broke forward at will and the Rangers fans were leaving in droves long before the final whistle. Johnston was nicknamed 'Magic' after the American basketball player of the same name. 'Why is he called Magic?' asked a joyous Hearts fan on a train which rocked back to Haymarket Station. 'Because he's just made 45,000 Rangers fans disappear!'

Hearts were never in relegation danger after that famous result although the unpredictable nature of following this damned team was never better illustrated when Partick Thistle came to Tynecastle and won 5-2 at the end of March. You just can't write a script when it comes to following the Hearts. Jim Jefferies was already looking to the following season when he signed Raith Rovers midfielder Colin Cameron. The Fifer had played in Rovers astonishing League Cup final triumph over Celtic a year before and his attacking prowess from midfield would give Hearts extra threat. Remarkably, after dropping to the foot of the table in October, Hearts revamped side ended the season in fourth place in the Premier Division. It had been a remarkable turnaround – and it wasn't over yet.

Hearts Scottish Cup run began with a home win over Partick Thistle before a difficult trip to Rugby Park to face Kilmarnock. A huge Hearts support headed for Ayrshire that day and they were instrumental in Hearts recording a 2-1 win thanks to a Neil Berry – yes, a Neil Berry – winner. More instrumental, however, was goalie Gilles Rousset who was in brilliant form that day. As the fans headed out of Rugby Park they bellowed 'Rousset – there's only one Rousset'. A love affair was born!

A Thursday night quarter final – yep, SKY Television again – at St. Johnstone saw Hearts edge home 2-1. Even better news was that Hearts avoided the Old Firm in the semi-final draw and faced Aberdeen at Hampden. Now, I'm not going to let my time spent in the Granite City cloud my judgement. Okay, maybe I will. But there's been an argument for several years now between Aberdonians and those in Edinburgh as to who is the larger club – Aberdeen or Hearts. The Aberdeen team of the 1980s was undoubtedly one of the greatest teams in Scottish football history. Equally, the Hearts team which lifted the league championship in 1958 by a record margin and with a record number of goals scored – 132 will never be beaten – is without peer. The argument rages on but it's worth looking at the average attendance of both teams in the last decade. And the attendance at the Scottish Cup semi-final of 1996 settled the debate in my book (well, this book) Just under 28,000 people went to Hampden – 20,000 sporting maroon and white. It was, however, a typical semi-final – awful. The only consolation for the huge Hearts support was that Allan Johnston headed home a John Robertson cross with a couple of minutes to go to give Hearts a 2-1 win – and a Scottish Cup final appearance beckoned for a club which had been on its knees a year before.

Thankfully, I'm at the end of this chapter, which means I can skip over the events of May 18th 1996. Rangers 5 Hearts 1. The fans new hero, Gilles Rousset, let a harmless shot slip through his fingers early in the second half to put Rangers 2-0 ahead and they never looked back. Enough said. But Gilles would get his own back two years later.

It had been a remarkable first season in charge for Jim Jefferies and his assistant Billy Brown. The rebuilding of Hearts was going apace. There were many more ups and downs ahead. But the excitement and pride of being a Hearts fan was back. And the reward for the most loyal supporters in the country was hovering into view.....

8

At Last! Glorious Hearts
1996-1998

Hearts greatest ever goalkeeper?
Antti Niemi

1996-1998

HOPE SPRINGS ETERNAL as the saying goes. The Scottish Cup Final of 1996 had been a bitter experience for all Hearts supporters and the pain of the humiliating 5-1 defeat was felt all through the summer. More than one Hibee asked if I had the time throughout the summer of 1996. 'I make it five past Rousset' was their gleeful reply. But given the awful start to the last league campaign, no one really thought Hearts would have been anywhere near Hampden and Jim Jefferies had achieved much in the twelve months he had been in charge at Tynecastle. However he knew further changes had to be made if Hearts were to continue to progress. Some of the players the manager had brought in, initially to steer Hearts away from relegation, were thanked, shaken by the hand and shown the way out of Tynecastle. Alan Lawrence, David Winnie and Hans Eskilsson had all served their purpose and most of the Tommy McLean signings such as Willie Jamieson, Craig Nelson and Brian Hamilton were also handed their P45s. Jefferies brought in much needed new blood. The capture of Dundee's Neil McCann, a winger who had been targeted by Celtic, was seen as a major coup for Jefferies as was the signing of Falkirk centre half Davie Weir. The Jefferies revolution was quickening.

But I wondered if the pace of this change was just a

little too quick. Hearts began season 1996/97 with a home game against Kilmarnock, which ended with a 3-2 victory thanks to two goals from youngster Paul Ritchie. Ritchie scored only very rarely for Hearts and when he did it was usually against Kilmarnock for some bizarre reason. A week later, though, Hearts slumped to a 4-0 loss at Pittodrie. As usual it took a trip to Easter Road to give Hearts the kick up the backside they needed and after failing to beat Dunfermline Athletic, Rangers or Motherwell, Jim Jefferies' team headed across Edinburgh in far from confident mood. Not that that ever mattered against the Leithers and two glorious goals from Colin Cameron and the inevitable counter from John Robertson gave Hearts a 3-1 win. 'Can you hear the Hibees sing?' we chanted heading along Albion Road. Can you ever?

Nonetheless, Hearts weren't quite making the progress we had all hoped for. Jim Jefferies was never averse to adding to the squad of players – a trait which would be his eventual undoing – but the likes of Darren Beckford, Jeremy Goss and Stephane Paille did little to enhance the squad, despite all three having decent reputations. Indeed Goss was a Welsh internationalist who played for Norwich City in their famous triumph over Bayern Munich in the Olympic Stadium a couple of years earlier but he never quite looked the part in a Hearts jersey. League form was patchy. Hearts went six games without a win and tension was beginning to mount once more. But three wins in succession over Christmas and New Year lifted spirits. The New Years Day Derby was at Easter Road and Hearts produced one of their finest performances against Hibernian in years – and there had been so many to choose from – to thrash the wee team 4-0 with new signing Jim Hamilton scoring twice. 'Happy New Year' bellowed the Hearts fans and it was the best possible start to 1997.

The first half of season 1996/97 was notable for a rare extended run in the League Cup, at that time sponsored by U.S. conglomerate Coca-Cola. The competition began with a home tie against Second Division Stenhousemuir. A warm August evening, the Edinburgh festival in full swing, the football season back, many fans in holiday mode, it was the perfect setting as we sat back and waited for the goal rush. Okay, I know, this is Hearts we're talking about. A club that never does things easily. After ninety minutes the score was 1-1. Yes, 1-1. Surely the part-timers legs would buckle during thirty minutes of extra time? Nope. Half an hour later it was still 1-1. A penalty shoot-out was required and Hearts record in these has never inspired much confidence. But this time, Jim Jefferies team squeezed through 5-4. It wasn't just the August weather that was making us sweat that night.

Extra-time was again required in the next round where many people fancied First Division St. Johnstone to cause an 'upset'. This time Hearts scored twice in the additional half-hour and so a quarter final with Celtic at Tynecastle beckoned. A tough enough task at the best of times but my statement about Hearts never doing things easily was never better illustrated than the week of this match. The previous Saturday, Hearts had been at Ibrox for a Premier League match and had lost 3-0. They weren't helped by an astonishing display of refereeing by Gerry Evans whose willingness to oblige the home team reached new heights when he sent off four – yes, four – Hearts players. Pasquelue Bruno, Neil Pointon, David Weir and Paul Ritchie were all sent for an early bath.

Indeed, had Hearts had one more player sent off, Mr Evans would have had to abandon the match as the rules of the game decrees that you must have at least seven players in your team. The Ibrox fiasco provoked outrage. At one stage, Chief Executive Chris Robinson appeared on the touchline and seemed to be signalling to the Hearts players to leave the field. Realising this would land Hearts in even deeper trouble than they were already in, manager Jim Jefferies waved his boss back to the stand and the game continued. When the furore died down, the subsequent suspensions meant Jefferies was left with almost an entire defence missing for the visit of Celtic in the League Cup.

Desperate times require desperate measures. Seventeen-year-old Gary Naysmith was brought in to make his first team debut. New signing Stefano Salvatori – how did you guess he was an Italian? – made his home debut and, in spite of him being a midfield player, played in defence. Most astonishing of all was the appearance of a complete stranger. Jeffries had secured the temporary signing – for one month only – of Wimbledon's Andy Thorn and the former Newcastle player went straight into the Hearts defence. Over 14,000 took their seats at Tynecastle fearing the worst. Just how could such a patched up team compete with Celtic? They soon got their answer. With Thorn and Salvatori in inspirational mood, Hearts absorbed huge Celtic pressure and were proving dangerous themselves on the counter-attack. Wave after wave of Celtic attacks were dispelled and Hearts went off to a standing ovation at half-time with the game still goalless. The second half followed a similar vein but such a brave performance looked doomed when Salvatori was sent off with twenty minutes to go – the fifth Hearts player red-carded in four days. But the fans roared their support and Hearts held out to force extra-time. Not before time, fate then smiled on Hearts as Celtic's Peter Grant was sent off in extra time and now the player parity was restored. Still Celtic pressed, still Hearts held out, doubtless willing to take their chances with a penalty shoot-out. But, with five minutes left, Hearts broke upfield with a speed, which astonished us all given the preceding 115 minutes. The ball broke to John Robertson on the edge of the penalty box and he drilled a powerful low shot past Celtic keeper Gordon Marshall to give Hearts a memorable victory over The Hoops. The scenes at the end of the game were as emotional as any I could remember at Tynecastle. Hearts had won a famous victory against all the odds. Now the semi-final beckoned.

First Division Dundee were the opponents at Easter Road but no one was taking them lightly. The Dees had reached the final the previous season and, given Hearts record in cup semi-finals against lower division opposition, I feared the worst. But Hearts survived a couple of nervy spells and secured a 3-1 win, the highlight being a glorious goal from Frenchman Stephane Paille. Six months after the Scottish Cup Final mauling, Hearts would face Rangers in a cup final again – this time the League Cup Final at Celtic Park as the national stadium was being rebuilt.

As we headed to Glasgow on a cold, snowy November afternoon our concerns increased the further west we travelled. The snow was becoming heavier and there were real doubts as to whether the game would go on. We sat in a car about a mile away from Celtic Park an hour before kick-off and listened to the radio. Snow swirled around us and my money was on us heading back home before three o'clock. But the game went ahead and, thankfully, the snow eased as the game kicked off.

With just twenty minutes gone we sat with hands clasped, praying for a blizzard, which would abandon the game. Hearts were already two goals behind, the second of which was clearly the fault of Pasquele Bruno who was daydreaming, allowing Ally McCoist to grab his second goal of the afternoon. The veteran striker gestured to the Hearts fans that it was too easy and, at that stage, it was. We feared another 5-1 drubbing. But Hearts kept at it and just before half-time Stevie Fulton was given time and space to turn in the penalty box and shoot past Andy Goram. 2-1, Hearts were back in it and when the second half began it was the maroon shirts that swarmed forward with Neil McCann in particular in devastating mood. His runs down the left wing had the Rangers defence chasing shadows and, at times, there were three Rangers players around the winger, trying to prise the ball from him. With just over an hour gone, McCann burst forward again before delivering an inch perfect cross to the head of John Robertson who glanced the ball past the flailing arms of Goram to level the scores at 2-2. Wee Robbo, who had endured so much heartbreak at Tynecastle, fell to the ground before being engulfed by joyous team mates. As the Hearts end went wild, I felt a lump in my throat. This was it, I thought. There was only one team in it and now the scores were level. Hearts were going to win a trophy!

Hearts kept coming forward in search of a third goal. It was one-way traffic with McCann tormentor in chief. A third goal duly arrived – but at the other end. John Robertson danced down the touchline and was clearly fouled. As the Hearts players stopped to prepare for a free-kick, the linesman kept his flag down and referee waved play on. Paul Gascoigne, the English enigma, skipped past three desperate Hearts challenges before despatching the ball past Gilles Rousset. 3-2 for Rangers. Fury on the Hearts bench and among the huge Hearts support. There was no way back. Gascoigne, as if to rub salt in the wounds, added a fourth and the chance of glory had disappeared again. Davie Weir headed in a third Hearts goal at the death but it was too little, too late. One of the best cup finals of recent years had ended Rangers 4 Hearts 3 and 20,000 thousand tearful Hearts fans gave their team an emotional standing ovation at the end of the match. Neil McCann gave one of the finest displays I've ever seen from a Hearts player and, in a major cup final, that was something to cherish.

Such dramatics were, sadly, not repeated in the Scottish Cup. After Cowdenbeath were thrashed 5-0 at Tynecastle, the fourth round saw Dundee United head for Tynecastle and a Jim Hamilton goal rescued a replay for Hearts. But the trip to Tannadice ended in a disappointing 1-0 defeat. For the second season running, Hearts ended fourth in the Premier Division but the end of the season proved highly emotional for one player. John Robertson had been seventeen years at Tynecastle and was Gorgie's favourite son. He was now nearing the end of his career but had the chance in the final league game of the season against Rangers at Tynecastle to become Hearts all time leading goalscorer. He had already equalled the legendary Jimmy Wardhaugh's record of 212 goals and needed just one more to set a new record and claim legendary status. When Hearts were awarded a penalty towards the end of the game there was only going to be one taker. Wee Robbo smashed the ball home and tearfully trotted back to the centre circle with almost the entire Hearts team on his back! As if to emphasis how special a player the wee fella is, Robbo added another sensational goal minutes later, skipping past two Rangers players on the edge of the penalty box before curling a truly magnificent left foot shot high into the net. This writer considers it a privilege to have seen probably the best centre forward Hearts have ever had – the legend that is John Robertson.

As season 1997/98 began, Jim Jefferies once again wheeled and dealt in the transfer market. Players such as Bruno, Goss and Beckford departed while it was the end of an era for long serving players such as Gary Mackay and John Colquhoun. Mackay, of a similar breed to John Robertson, clocked up a record number 737 appearances for Hearts and the midfield player is another who Hearts fans have attired legendary status. Mackay was loyal to Hearts for nearly twenty years, a loyalty that simply won't be repeated given the state of the game in the 21st century. Two additions to the Hearts team were Austrian Thomas Flogel and French striker Stephane Adam. Flogel made his debut in the opening league game at Ibrox, unusual for the fact that the game was played on a Monday night. Yes, live television dictated again and who cared if this dramatically affected the size of the travelling support? Certainly not the television people. Flogel had a nightmarish first half and was replaced by Adam and the 3-1 defeat by the champions was not unexpected. But the first indications that this was to become a special season for Hearts came a week later when Aberdeen came to Tynecastle.

If you want to end up with egg all over your face, the

sure-fire way to do it is to slag off your opponents on the eve of a game. Aberdeen striker Dean Windass scoffed at Hearts stated target of being the third best team in Scotland i.e. the best after the Old Firm. Windass declared that Aberdeen were more ambitious, looking for top spot and would be happy to leave Hearts languishing in third. Jim Jefferies duly pinned press statements attributed to Windass on the dressing room walls and, despite falling behind to an early Mike Newell goal, Hearts proceeded to destroy Aberdeen 4-1 with a fine display of attacking football. Windass was strangely quiet after the game.

Hearts lost to Dunfermline Athletic but then embarked on a remarkable run which produced the finest spell of football seen at Tynecastle since the halcyon days of the 1950s. Hearts won eleven out of their next twelve games – the one defeat coming at Celtic Park – and suddenly were challenging the Old Firm at the top of the table. There were some stunning performances as Hearts won 4-1 at Motherwell, defeated Kilmarnock 5-3 at Tynecastle – Stephane Adam scoring a hat-trick – and repeated their 4-1 Tynecastle scoreline at Pittodrie where Aberdeen were demolished once again. With Colin Cameron and born-again Stevie Fulton dictating midfield, Paul Ritchie and Davie Weir rock solid at the back and Stephane Adam, Neil McCann and John Robertson scoring freely up front, Hearts were setting the league on fire. However, just before Christmas, a 5-2 defeat at home to Rangers brought realism back into the fray and the New Year Derby against Hibernian at Tynecastle was hard to take. No, of course Hearts didn't lose, but having been 2-0 ahead after just five minutes thanks to two Stevie Fulton goals, Hearts fans were gleefully rubbing their hands in anticipation of handing the wee team a severe drubbing. Instead, they let Hibs back into the game and it ended 2-2 – a dent to Hearts championship hopes.

Yes, Hearts were in with a shout of the league title – an alien concept certainly but one which was realistic in the early months of 1998. From the 5-2 defeat by Rangers in December, Hearts went unbeaten until April including securing draws at Ibrox and Celtic Park. Indeed, only a Jorg Albertz equaliser in the dying seconds rescued a point for Rangers, denying Hearts a famous win. But as Celtic, Rangers and Hearts headed for home in the championship race, it was Hearts who fell at the final fence. On April 8th, Motherwell came to a rain-soaked Tynecastle and defended robustly for a 1-1 draw. That opened up a gap between the Old Firm and Hearts which was never going to be closed. All hopes of a recovery disappeared completely when Hearts lost 2-1 to Hibernian at Easter Road three days later despite John Robertson's goal during an April snow shower. Ignorant Hibees chanted 'you're going tae win **** all' but Hearts fans responded with an old wartime favourite 'We'll Meet Again, Don't Know Where, Don't Know When' – a painful reminder to those Hibees that if your team is at the bottom of the league then relegation usually follows. As it did for Edinburgh's second team in May 1998. A glorious month as it turned out.

Hearts ended the league season in a highly creditable third place, just seven points behind champions Rangers and a startling seventeen points ahead of fourth placed Kilmarnock. Oh, incidentally, Dean Windass's Aberdeen finished sixth – just nine points clear of the relegation spot. But if Hearts league form stumbled, their progress in the Scottish Cup did anything but. If truth were told it had been a relatively straightforward path to the final. Lower league opposition in the shape of Clydebank, now sadly defunct, Albion Rovers and Ayr United were all beaten at Tynecastle without too much difficulty. They say you need luck to win trophies and the cup draws were certainly kind to Hearts, giving them home draws all the way. Even when the semi-final draw was made, Hearts were paired with First Division Falkirk while the Old Firm clashed in the other semi-final. Falkirk had been beaten finalists eleven months earlier when they lost the 1997 final 1-0 to Kilmarnock and with former Jambo Neil Berry in their defence were fired up for giving Hearts a tough time in the match played at Ibrox. Stephane Adam gave Hearts an early lead but the match was then dominated by Falkirk and we all sat uneasily as the game drew to its conclusion. When former Hibee Kevin McAllister scored a wonder goal to tie the scores with fifteen minutes left, we all feared the worst. Was Hearts semi-final hoodoo about to strike again? We got the answer in injury time. Neil McCann left Neil Berry for dead and crossed into the penalty box for Stephane Adam to score his second. 2-1 for Hearts and McCann added a third for good measure seconds later. 3-1 and Hearts were in their second Scottish Cup Final in two years. Again they would face Rangers. Again at Celtic Park. But this time there would be a different, more glorious outcome!

May 16th 1998. A date synonymous with glory for all Hearts supporters.

Rangers manager Walter Smith had announced in October that he intended to quit at the end of the season and this appeared to unsettle the club. Rangers slipped in the league and, in February, were trailing both Celtic and Hearts. Scottish Cup progress was stuttering but they made it to the final after rivals Celtic were defeated in a pulsating semi-final at Celtic Park to set up the sequel to the 1996 final.

Even Rangers conceded that Hearts were a much-improved team from the one that capitulated two years earlier but Walter Smith's side were still firm favourites for the trophy. More than 48,000 supporters headed for Celtic Park on a warm May afternoon to witness one of the most emotional cup finals in years. This was the Hearts team that would create history that memorable afternoon:

Hearts: Rousset; McPherson; Naysmith; Weir; Salvatori; Ritchie; McCann; Fulton; Adam; Cameron; Flogel. Substitutes: Hamilton, Robertson; Murray.

Referee: W. Young

It was a sign of the cosmopolitan times that, of the Rangers side, only Gordon Durie and Ian Ferguson were born in Scotland (Richard Gough was born in Stockholm while Andy Goram and Stuart McCall were born in England of Scottish parentage). Even the Hearts side contained two Frenchmen, an Italian and an Austrian.

Both sides were affected by pre-match blows. Rangers influential German, Jorg Albertz was sent off for violent conduct the previous week at Tannadice while injury ruled out Swede Jonas Thern. Hearts captain Gary Locke, who was stretchered off injured after just seven minutes during the 1996 final, missed the '98 final because of a hamstring injury and, being a Hearts daft youngster, his anguish was felt by every Hearts supporter.

Rangers-Hearts Scottish Cup finals have a history of

having remarkable beginnings. The 1976 final between the pair began at two minutes to three, Rangers scored within eighty seconds, and so Hearts were a goal behind before the official kick-off time! Astonishingly, the 1996 final kicked off at a minute to three and Hearts lost their captain within seven minutes. We wondered what the 1998 final would have in store – we got our answer after barely a minute!

From the kick-off Hearts stormed upfield. Stand-in captain Steve Fulton burst into the Rangers penalty box only to be halted by Ian Ferguson. Halted illegally said referee Young and he awarded a penalty to Hearts. From my seat at the other end of the stadium, it looked like the foul had been committed outside the penalty box but, tellingly, few Rangers players protested. Colin Cameron stepped up to slot the penalty kick beyond goalkeeper Andy Goram and Hearts had a sensational lead after just eighty seconds. Hearts fans erupted in the Celtic Park cauldron and it was certainly a start to the match few people – even in Edinburgh – had predicted. I had never known what it was like to see my team ahead in a cup final but the nerves in my stomach wouldn't let me savour the moment!

Rangers, although stung by such an early setback, responded. Rino Gattuso embarked on a powerful run from midfield, which ended with a shot, which was comfortably saved by Rousset. Then Brian Laudrup had an effort which was blocked by nineteen year old Gary Naysmith. Hearts, however, weren't just sitting back. Despite a significant change in tactics by Jim Jefferies which saw the team adapt a more rigid 4-4-2 formation rather than their normal swashbuckling style of 4-3-3, the maroons were still capable of lightening raids on the break, epitomised by young Naysmith who was having an outstanding game at full back. The Scotland Under 21 star had just been named Young Player of the Year and his assured defending and attacking abilities were there for all to see at Celtic Park.

After half an hour Rangers Ian Ferguson – a veteran of St. Mirren's cup triumph in 1987 – was put through by Laudrup but pulled his effort wide. Then came Rangers best effort thus far. Accepting a short free kick some thirty-five yards out, Lorenzo Amoruso fired in a magnificent shot which appeared to be heading for the top left hand corner of the net. But as Rangers prepared to celebrate the equaliser Hearts keeper Gilles Rousset leapt majestically to palm the ball past the post. It was a fantastic save and a defining moment. In the 1996 final, the big Frenchman let a shot slip through his fingers to give Rangers a two-goal advantage from which they never looked back. It was a schoolboy error and Rousset hid his face behind his hands at the realisation at what he had done. But now, two years later, he produced one of the great stops and the twenty three thousand Hearts supporters stood to acclaim the moment. Half-time arrived with Hearts still ahead and I wondered if history was about to be made.

At the start of the second half Rangers replaced the unhappy Stensaas with the veteran campaigner that was Ally McCoist. It signalled an all-out attacking policy by Walter Smith and for the opening five minutes of the second period Hearts were pinned back in their own half. Within minutes McCoist received a pass from the tireless Brian Laudrup but his effort went into the side net. Urged on by captain Richard Gough -playing his last game for the Ibrox club – Rangers swept forward and one wondered if Hearts could hold out. But, on fifty-three minutes, the Hearts support erupted once more. Gilles Rousset launched a long ball down field and it seemed that Rangers defender Lorenzo Amoruso would clear the danger. But the Italian dithered as he went to strike the ball and Frenchman Stephane Adam nipped in behind him. Taking the ball into the penalty box, Adam fired in a powerful shot which goalkeeper Goram could only parry into the net. 2-0 to Hearts and Adam ran with outstretched arms to an ecstatic Jambos support to milk the celebrations. Complete strangers danced with each other in the aisles of Celtic Park. A beer-bellied, hairy, foul-breathed Hearts fan jumped on my back. But not even she could quell my joy......

The noise from the Hearts end was deafening. Was the dream about to come true? Was thirty-six years of anguish about to end? We had been kicked in the teeth so often by countless near misses from this bloody team of ours. I could scarcely believe it. But there were still thirty-five minutes to go. And a wounded Rangers side is when they are at their most dangerous. Seconds later Hearts almost ended the argument when Thomas Flogel headed a Steve Fulton free-kick powerfully towards goal but his effort was well saved by Goram. And, inevitably, Rangers stormed back.

Ally McCoist, despite being written off by some people at 35 years of age, was proving a real handful for the youthful Hearts defence. A snap shot from the striker from just six yards out was well saved by Rousset before the former Sunderland player appeared to be fouled by Dave McPherson. Time was running out for Rangers but with nine minutes to go, McCoist finally got the goal both he and his side deserved. Ferguson played the ball forward to Gattuso. The Italian slipped it to McCoist who drove the ball past Rousset and into the net from eighteen yards.

The last few minutes of the 1998 Scottish Cup final were tense, nervous and fraught for supporters of both sides. Rangers threw everything at the Hearts defence but Jim Jefferies' side scented glory. But there was still time for more drama in this epic cup final. With two minutes to go, McCoist went down in the penalty box after a foul by David Weir. Referee Young immediately blew his whistle. For a moment it looked like a penalty to Rangers. Were Hearts hopes to be cruelly dashed once more? After a nod from the assistant referee, Willie Young awarded a free-kick on the edge of the penalty box much to the disgust of McCoist. Brian Laudrup's free-kick was deflected wide and we breathed a huge sigh of relief. The period of injury time seemed to last forever. Fully four minutes stoppage time had been played when, at last, referee Young blew for the end of the match. The Hearts support roared themselves hoarse and danced for joy. Jim Jefferies almost crushed his assistant Billy Brown with a hug of delight. Hearts had won the Scottish Cup for the first time since 1956 and four decades of heartbreak had come to an end.

The scenes which followed at Celtic Park were remarkable. Grown men wept and the tide of emotion that washed over those in maroon seemed almost to overpower them. Veteran striker John Robertson, a substitute but who never came on, was clearly overcome. 'Robbo' had been at the club for seventeen years but had yet to win a medal with the club he loved. Now, in his last season at Tynecastle, his dream had come true as it had for the thousands of jubilant supporters who found it difficult to comprehend just what had happened. When Steve Fulton went to collect the trophy he invited club captain Gary Locke to go up with him. The injured Locke didn't need to be asked twice and the two players held the cup aloft to a huge ovation from the Hearts support.

Edinburgh partied all weekend as the players paraded the cup through the streets of the famous old city and on to Tynecastle Stadium for a truly emotional home-coming. An estimated one hundred thousand Hearts fans welcomed them home and Edinburgh let down it's collective hair. Manager Jim Jefferies had said before the game that the players could become legends if they won the cup and there's little doubt that the Hearts support treated their heroes in a way befitting such a status.

It was an emotional end to an emotional season. It was made all the sweeter by the sight of Hibs plummeting to the foot of the table after a disastrous run of results. Manager Jim Duffy was sacked to be replaced by Alex McLeish but the damage had already been done. Hibs were relegated at the end of the season.

It's true to say that Hearts had become something of a laughing stock in Scottish football as a result of their lack of success and their almost constant failure to produce the goods when it really mattered. Season 1997-98 changed all that. Throughout the season Hearts had consistently produced a sparkling brand of fluent, attacking football which delighted the purists. They had given the Old Firm the fright of their lives in the race for the league title.

And, after thirty-six years of hurt, they had finally brought silverware back to Tynecastle. The glory days were back. We were all sure of that.....

9

Levein the Past Behind
1998-2003

Captain Marvel - Hearts skipper for
the new millennium, Steven Pressley

1998-2003

THE SUMMER OF 1998 was a memorable one. None of the born again Hearts supporters wanted it to end. We bored everyone rigid with tales of the Cup Final, how Hearts were winners again and how we were going to challenge for the league championship once more. Jim Jefferies had already planned ahead by signing centre half Steven Pressley from Dundee United and former Motherwell left back Rab Mackinnon from Twente Enschede. Hearts fans tormented supporters of the wee team, about to get even smaller as life in the First Division beckoned for Hibernian. Tell me, my little Hibby friend, who's playing at Easter Road this week? Stranraer eh? All ticket is it? Hang on, I must go and change these trousers....

The summer of 1998 also saw the World Cup in France. Scotland had the honour of playing the first game of the tournament – unfortunately, it was against the holders Brazil. Ronaldo and co. managed to fend off the likes of Darren Jackson and won 2-1 but Scotland had played creditably. When John Collins equalised with a penalty kick early in the second half, I wondered if my football life was ever going to top this. Hearts had won the Scottish Cup and now Scotland had a better than evens chance of beating Brazil in the World Cup. But it wasn't to be. Scotland drew their next game with Norway then capitulated to Morocco by 3-0 and, once again, the

Scots were home before the postcards.

Season 1997/98 had seen Hearts kick off against Rangers on a Monday night. Twelve months later, Rangers were again the first match opponents in the league. This time the game was at Tynecastle. On that traditional kick-off time – five past six on a Sunday evening. Yet again, satellite television was dictating the kick-off times. But this was ridiculous. Tynecastle was less than full for the fixture, which, being the first home game since the Cup triumph, was something of a disappointment to Chris Robinson and the board of directors. But it was hardly surprising – Sunday evening is not a time for football. But the perceived lack of response from fans sowed the seeds of doubt in the mind of the Chief Executive as to whether Hearts could genuinely challenge the Old Firm. The game itself was a riveting affair. Rangers had a new manager – former Dutch Coach Dick Advocaat – in charge but it was Hearts who picked up where they had left off from the previous glorious season. Stephane Adam and Jim Hamilton scored two goals in the opening half an hour and the Hearts support revelled in the jubilation. Hearts held on to win 2-1 and we all looked forward to another tumultuous season. 'You Never Won F*** All' we taunted the bemused Rangers support (leaving aside the obvious grammatical failings) And what happens when Hearts fans get too full of themselves? Yes – read on if you can...

With that memorable opening day win we all hoped that Hearts would scale the heights of the previous campaign – and even higher. I should have known better but the cup win had given me a feeling of grandeur. Four thousand Hearts fans headed for Tannadice and a goal-less draw against Dundee United was disappointing, given the standards this Hearts team had set themselves. It was a sign of the times though that the home support, in between berating former hero Steven Pressley, gave their team a standing ovation at the end of the game. It showed how far Hearts had come – considerably further than Hibernian who had lost at home that weekend 2-1 to Stranraer in the First Division. Most certainly the nadir of Alex McLeish's management. Hearts defeated Aberdeen at Tynecastle the following week but the performance was not inspiring. And the first signs of alarm came the following week at Rugby Park when Hearts lost 3-0 to an Ally McCoist inspired Kilmarnock. When Dundee then won at Tynecastle and Hearts struggled to a 1-1 draw at Dunfermline it seemed our dance with glory had come to an end. Then Jim Hamilton scored in a 1-1 draw at Celtic Park and we consoled ourselves that the last few weeks had just been a blip. Not so. Hearts lost to Rangers and the two Dundee clubs and faint hopes of challenging for the league championship were snuffed out well before Christmas. Irritation with what had turned sour turned to real anger in the League Cup semi-final with St. Johnstone at Easter Road. Hearts fans wore smug grins when the semi-final draw was made. Wow, another cup final appearance beckoning – our fourth in two and a half years. Wouldn't the S.F.A. be tired of yet another Rangers-Hearts cup final?! But on a woeful October night at the ground of Hibernian, Hearts fans illusions were shattered for good. St. Johnstone played Hearts off the park and cantered to an easy 3-0 win. It could – and should – have been more. Hearts fans trooped out of Easter Road angry. Something had happened at Tynecastle and we all wanted to know what. Defeat was bad enough but the manner of the defeat was unacceptable – it seemed to this disbelieving onlooker that some of the players weren't trying. Perhaps the hunger to succeed had gone. But it would all soon become painfully apparent.

After Celtic were beaten 2-1 at Tynecastle at the beginning of December – it was truly bizarre that Hearts couldn't beat the Hoops the previous season but were running up impressive results this time round – Hearts supporters were given devastating news on the eve of the visit of Rangers just before Christmas. Neil McCann, a mainstay of the team that had tasted glory, had been transferred to Rangers for just £1.5m. I was numb at the news. McCann was perhaps Hearts best player. His mercurial runs at defenders were a joy to see. He produced a 'Johan Cruyff' moment against Aberdeen the season before when he turned two defenders with a deft shimmy that had the Hearts supporters on their feet in admiration. Now, not only was he leaving Hearts, but also he would be coming back to Tynecastle wearing the blue of Rangers. Why? It turned out McCann had a clause in his contract that stated if a bigger club came in for him he could leave. And the ridiculous transfer fee was all that Rangers were going to offer. Hearts lost to Rangers, Aberdeen, Kilmarnock and Dundee. Then Davie Weir jumped ship and headed for Everton. The cup winning team was breaking up much sooner – too much sooner – than we thought. At this stage, Jim Jefferies seemed to panic. Former French internationalist Vincent Guerin signed on a short-term deal but he clearly wasn't the player he used to be – why would he be signing for Hearts if he were? Gary McSwegan signed from Dundee United, Lee Makel came from Huddersfield Town and Spanish winger Juanjo arrived from Barcelona. On top of players leaving, Hearts suffered an injury crisis over Christmas and New Year. Centre forward Derek Lilley, once of Morton, was hurriedly signed on loan from Leeds United and, indeed, scored against Dundee at Tynecastle – but Hearts still lost 2-1. And were now slipping down the league table at a frightening rate of knots.

Despite the arrival of Lilley, McSwegan and Juanjo, Hearts entered a horrendous spell when they couldn't score a league goal to save themselves – literally. Hopes that defending the Scottish Cup would spark a revival crashed when Hearts lost in the third round, 3-1 at Motherwell. Another night of bitter disappointment. In the league, Hearts went six long games without even scoring a goal. Inevitably, they plunged to the foot of the league table. Astonishingly, agonisingly, ten months after lifting the Scottish Cup, Hearts were staring relegation in the face. A 2-0 defeat by Dundee at the end of March was pitiful. I left the ground that day almost as shell-shocked as when I left the same ground thirteen years earlier having seen Hearts lose the league. Hearts were truly awful. I just couldn't see how relegation could be avoided. By now Jim Jefferies had tried so many new faces it was getting to be almost an embarrassment. Anyone who witnessed a player called Mo Berthe making his Hearts debut at Dens Park that day must have thought they were in a time warp and it was 1978. Only Hearts could take you from the heights of ecstasy to the depths of despair in less than a year. Then three things happened.

Firstly, nine months after playing for Scotland against Brazil in the World Cup of 1998, Celtic's Darren Jackson signed for Hearts for a fee in excess of £300,000. It was a sanguine moment. Jackson had suffered a major health scare earlier in the season and consequently found it difficult to get back into Celtic's first team. Despite his history – he was a former Hibernian favourite – Jackson was exactly the type of player Hearts needed to rescue them from the abyss. Secondly, Colin Cameron, a pivotal influence on the Hearts team returned from a lengthy injury lay-off. 'Mickey' had been out for months and his presence in the team had been sorely missed. Thirdly, striker Gary McSwegan – having not scored in the four months since joining the club – suddenly discovered the knack of putting the ball in the net. McSwegan scored twice in a 2-2 draw with Kilmarnock and Hearts headed for Tannadice on a Tuesday night in April knowing a win would lift them off the bottom of the league. Despite losing a goal in the opening five minutes, Hearts stormed back. McSwegan unleashed a ferocious twenty five yard screamer which flew into the net for the equaliser, nodded Hearts in front before half-time and then watched Colin Cameron score a sublime third to seal three crucial points. The maroon army of travelling Hearts fans roared their approval and sang the tune of that marvellous Steve McQueen film 'The Great Escape'. A fortnight later, Hearts cruised to a 4-0 win at Motherwell before hitting another four against Dundee United at Tynecastle. Darren Jackson was immense during this revitalised period and safety from demotion was assured when Dunfermline Athletic were beaten 2-0 at Tynecastle on a Bank Holiday Monday. A relaxed Hearts then scored five goals against Aberdeen at Pittodrie on the final day of the season. I met an old Aberdonian pal as I headed out of the ground and I reverted to the gloating mode of a year before. But, in truth, season 1998/99 was almost too much to bear.

Perhaps it had something to do with the fact that Hearts were back in European competition. You may have noticed in this book that Hearts tend to struggle domestically when European games appear in the fixture list. Hearts defeated Estonians Lantana home and away in the preliminary round of the Cup Winners Cup and, inevitably, were handed a tough draw in the first round proper. Real Mallorca weren't one of the bigger names in Spanish football but clearly able enough to have lifted the Spanish Cup. A 1-0 win for the Spaniards in the first leg at Tynecastle seemed to signal the end of another Hearts campaign in Europe but the second leg on the holiday island turned out to be a remarkable affair. Hearts were unhappy even before a ball was kicked in anger. It appeared the size of the goalposts were not of the required standard for U.E.F.A. and Chief Executive Chris Robinson clearly felt something underhand was going on. Hearts protested to U.E.F.A. but played the game anyway. Mallorca went ahead but Jim Hamilton scored an equaliser and the Spaniards were hanging on at the end for another Hearts goal would have put Jim Jefferies team through on the away goals rule. But the match ended 1-1 and yet another hard luck story entered the annuls of this beloved club of ours.

It's fair to say I wasn't sure what to expect when season 1999/2000 kicked off at McDiarmid Park. Hearts began as impressively as they had the previous season and thrashed St. Johnstone 4-1 with Darren Jackson again outstanding. The Hibees were back in the Premier League having won the First Division at a canter and manager Alex McLeish had transformed the club. Hearts drew 1-1 at Easter Road in the first Edinburgh derby for almost eighteen months and it would be almost a complete season before we would taste victory over the wee team. Two heavy defeats were inflicted from the Old Firm and results in the first half of the season were mixed although, thankfully, the traumas of the previous season were avoided for the most part. I say for the most part because the week before Christmas, Hibernian came to Tynecastle and won 3-0. A rank awful performance from Hearts – I was drowning my sorrows in the Station Tavern when Kenny Miller scored Hibs third goal. It was Hearts heaviest defeat at home from Hibs since a certain game in 1973 and it was a bitter pill to swallow.

Soon after came an announcement that would, ultimately cause much angst at Tynecastle. Chris Robinson had secured a major financial investment from the Scottish Media Group. £8m was to be 'invested' by the group who controlled Scottish Television and The Herald newspaper among others. Half of the money was immediately ring-fenced for Hearts ambitious plans for a youth academy while the other half was given to manager Jim Jefferies to restructure the playing squad. For the first time in his managerial career, Jefferies had money to spend on players and this was to prove the acid test for the former Falkirk manager. He spent £400,000 on a new goalkeeper – Antti Niemi signed from Rangers and was to go on to attain legendary status among the Hearts support. Other signings were not so successful. Gordan Petric, a centre half formerly of Rangers and Dundee United was signed from Crystal Palace. Petric was believed by many to have signed a lucrative contract at Tynecastle to become the club's highest paid player. Jefferies also signed Fitzroy Simpson – whose last visit to Tynecastle had been with Manchester City who lost a pre-season friendly 5-1 – and Robert Tomascheck, the

Slovakian captain. What the manager wasn't aware of was that the money he was given to spend on new players also included a budget for their wages. Hearts were back on the slippery slope and, crucially, the players Jefferies had brought in – Niemi apart – were not performing they way Hearts hoped they would.

The emergence of Scott Severin as a player of some merit in midfield was at least something to be thankful for but the season wasn't particularly going anywhere when Hearts headed for Celtic Park in February 2000. As happens all too frequently at Celtic Park, Celtic raced into an early two goal lead and Hearts fans crossed their arms and gritted their teeth in anticipation of another humping in Glasgow's East End. But, Colin Cameron pulled a goal back just before half-time and this was enough to sow seeds of doubt into the minds of the home team. Gary Naysmith scored a majestic equaliser early in the second half before Colin Cameron slotted home a penalty kick ten minutes before the end to give Hearts an unlikely 3-2 win. I couldn't remember the last time Hearts had scored three goals against Celtic at Celtic Park and certainly not winning after being two goals down. Celtic's faux pas was completed four days later when they lost at home to Inverness Caledonian Thistle in the Scottish Cup and their Head Coach John Barnes was on his way out.

Towards the end of the season we had the indignity of another defeat by Hibernian, 3-1 at Easter Road. But Hearts had huffed and puffed their way through the season and required a win on the final day of the league campaign to clinch a place in the U.E.F.A Cup. And our opponents at Tynecastle on that final day? Erm, Hibernian. But if there was ever a time to record a win over the wee team this was it and Hearts duly won 2-1 thanks to a fine goal from Juanjo and another from McSwegan. What better way to end the season than to beat your rivals and qualify for Europe at the same time? Scottish Cup hopes were ended on a Sunday evening at Ibrox when Rangers, backed by their delightful supporters, won 4-1. I took my thirteen-year-old daughter to that game and she was 'treated' to the sight of a Rangers fan dropping his trousers at frequent intervals. When I complained to Glasgow's 'other' boys in blue – the renowned 'polis' – I was told if I didn't like it then I didn't have to come. Thanks, boys.

So what would season 2000/2001 bring? A new millennium, same old stuff as before? Well, yep, the latter. Four out the first five league games were draws – shades of 1976 for emotionally scarred Hearts fans like me. And we also had European competition in the shape of the U.E.F.A. Cup. Icelandic opposition IVB were beaten home and away in much the same manner as Lantana had been a year earlier. But, again, in the first round proper Hearts were given tough opponents. German side VFB Stuttgart were considered by many to be dark horses for the competition – just our luck we draw them in the first round then. The first leg in Stuttgart was a backs-to-the-wall performance that saw Hearts head home with a 1-0 defeat. Well a packed Tynecastle would be worth a goal of a start wouldn't it? Normally, yes. But Tynecastle wasn't quite packed. Less than 14,500 attended the game. Part of the reason for this was Hearts bowing to the financial inducement from German television and agreeing to the game kicking off in Gorgie at 9.00 p.m. on a Thursday night. Quite. There was still a decent atmosphere though and Steven

Pressley, Gordan Petric and Colin Cameron scored as Hearts led 3-2 in the dying minutes. The Germans stood to go through on the away goals rule when Petric found himself alone in the Stuttgart penalty box with just the goalkeeper to beat. After taking the ball on his chest, the centre half let the ball bounce before rifling a right foot shot past the Stuttgart goalkeeper........past the crossbar, past most of the supporters in the Gorgie Stand and, for all I know, the ball may have landed on the roof of a number three bus to Dalkeith. The final whistle blew soon after. Another glorious failure to add to a history of glorious failures.

In the league Hearts defeated Motherwell 3-0 and then thrashed Dundee United 4-0 at Tannadice and things looked good for the trip to Easter Road in October. Things looked even better when Ulsterman Andy Kirk gave Hearts the lead five minutes before half-time. But Hibernian replied with two quick goals – before the roof fell in on Hearts spectacularly in the second half. Inspired by Russell Latapy, Hibs raced into a 6-1 lead with minutes to go. Colin Cameron pulled one back in the dying seconds but the goal was greeted by sarcastic cheers from the home support – the away end had emptied long before. 6-2 is a crushing defeat at any time. Against Hibernian it's akin to the end of the world. The game was played on a Sunday night to suit the SKY television audience and there were angry scenes outside Tynecastle as the players and officials returned there around 9.00 p.m. For the first time, there were chants of Jefferies Must Go from angry Hearts fans although most of the resentment was directed towards Chief Executive Chris Robinson and the board of directors who had already angered the fans by selling full back Gary

Naysmith to Everton a few weeks earlier. It was believed that Naysmith didn't want to go, happy as he was living in Midlothian and being Hearts daft. But he didn't appear to have a choice and another of the cup winning team was on his way.

A week later St. Johnstone came to Tynecastle and won 3-0. All too easily. This time there were several hundred supporters at the back of the main stand after the game with the same chants and demands as the previous Sunday, only this time more vociferous. A 5-2 defeat by Celtic at Tynecastle in the League Cup added to the woe and although Aberdeen and St. Mirren were defeated it was clear the end was in sight for the manager. Hearts insisted that Jim Jefferies chose to resign from the manager's job at Tynecastle although rumour and counter rumour suggested he was sacked and given a huge pay-off to remain silent. No one knew for sure. Assistant Billy Brown was sacked – the club made that perfectly clear. It merely added to the confusion. Assistant Coach Peter Houston took temporary charge of first team affairs and it was probably the worst time to head for Celtic Park. A 6-1 thrashing from Celtic, now managed by Martin O'Neill, merely confirmed this. The dark skies had returned to Tynecastle and the grapevine resounded to countless stories about what had happened. Some Hearts supporters were angry that a man who had ended thirty six barren years by delivering the Scottish Cup on that memorable day in 1998 should be treated this way. Even if he had resigned, they said, surely the board of directors should have been doing all they could to keep him?

My own view was that it was time for a change. Yes, Jim Jefferies had been good for Hearts, yes he had delivered the much yearned for trophy. But there were signs, particularly in his final two years at Tynecastle that Hearts were going backwards. Some of Jefferies signings beggared belief – the capture of Antti Niemi being his last piece of really good business in my view. The team tactics seemed now to resort to a dreary long ball game and the lack of creativity in midfield was alarming. In my opinion, Jefferies was too loyal to some players with the likes of Gary Locke and Stevie Fulton, both passionate and committed players, appearing as regulars no matter their form. It was the end of an era – but it was an era that was never going to end easily.

But who would replace Jim Jefferies? There were two obvious candidates. Sandy Clark had transformed St. Johnstone and had taken them to the League Cup final and into the U.E.F.A. Cup, a feat last achieved by the Perth club nearly three decades earlier. However, Chris Robinson's first act as Chief Executive when he took over in 1994 was to sack the Hearts manager – who happened to be Sandy Clark. Quotes have been attributed to Clark saying he was keen on a move back to Tynecastle but his wife advised him against it. Once bitten as the saying goes...

The other candidate was a promising young manager, still learning his trade. In 1983 Hearts signed a young centre half from Cowdenbeath and marked him as one for the future. Seventeen years later Hearts went back to the Blue Brazil and signed the same man – as Head Coach. Craig Levein served Hearts with distinction as a player until injury forced him to retire prematurely in 1995. Back then, at a tearful press conference, Levein said he hoped one day to return to Tynecastle as manager. After a successful spell at Cowdenbeath – where his team would eventually gain promotion to the Second Division – Levein did indeed return to Tynecastle under the title of Head Coach, with Peter Houston appointed Assistant Coach.

Many Hearts supporters, while appreciating Levein's undoubted talents as a player, doubted if he was ready to make a managerial move to one of the country's leading clubs. Some saw Levein as a 'yes man' dancing to the Chief Executive's tune. Levein angrily responded that he was his own man and he would build a new Hearts his way. His immediate target, however, was to cut the spiralling wage bill.

Levein's first game in charge was at home to Rangers in December. Inevitably, Hearts lost 1-0 but there were signs, even in that first game, that Levein wanted the team to adopt a more thoughtful approach, to build from the back, a more patient style. The results on the pitch weren't exactly spectacular and the first signs that Levein could indeed be an angry man came in January at Pittodrie when Hearts lost tamely to a distinctly average Aberdeen team. The new Head Coach described some of his players as thieves after the game for having the nerve to claim their wages and his comments did not go down well with some of the more established playing staff. The team stuttered through the depths of winter but it all came good in a game in early February when Dunfermline Athletic came to Tynecastle. It was one of those days when it seemed every time Hearts went up the park they scored. Hearts were 4-0 up at half-time and we munched our pies content that not even Hearts could throw away a four goal lead. This was emphasised when Stephane Adam scored right from the kick-off at the start of the second half and Hearts eventually won 7-1. They were 7-1 ahead with almost twenty minutes still remaining but no one complained about the lack of goal-mouth action in the final quarter! A mini revival was on the cards and, remarkably, Hearts were on the verge of clinching an unlikely U.E.F.A. Cup place going into the final game of the season. Hearts had to beat Dundee at Tynecastle and hope Euro rivals Kilmarnock would lose at home. As Killie were playing league champions Celtic, we kept our fingers crossed. But, with the championship already won, Celtic boss Martin O'Neill played what amounted to a reserve team and Killie won 1-0 to pinch the U.E.F.A. Cup spot from under the noses of Hearts who beat Dundee 2-0.

Hearts had what you could call a typical maroon Scottish Cup campaign. A replay was required to over-come Second Division Berwick Rangers (and when the English side went ahead in the replay at Tynecastle we had a nervous hour or so) and another replay was needed to beat Dundee who drew 1-1 in Gorgie but succumbed to a superb Robert Tomaschek goal in the replay at Dens Park. Hearts quarter final opponents? Celtic. At Celtic Park. Yes, you know the script – Hearts lost 1-0 in a game that was shown live on the BBC.

It was clearly going to be the end of the road for many of the Hearts squad. Craig Levein wanted to build his own side. Robert Tomaschek, Darren Jackson and Gary Locke left Tynecastle while it's fair comment to say Hearts fans were glad to see the back of Gordan Petric who was understood to be the club's highest earner but who, in the eyes of this writer, certainly didn't merit the accolade. Others followed notably Juanjo and Gary McSwegan who had a major row with Craig Levein and was banned from training with the first team. The former

Rangers striker was effectively an outcast and few tears were shed when he eventually teamed up again with Jim Jefferies who had now taken over at Kilmarnock. Levein brought in Steven Boyack, Kevin McKenna and Austin McCann before two pieces of business showed the Head Coach had a shrewd an eye for talent as anyone in the country. Jamaican internationalist Riccardo Fuller would sign for Hearts on loan midway through season 2001/2002 and he was to prove a massive hit with the supporters during his brief spell in Gorgie. Fuller possessed immense skill and showed great strength and his trickery on the ball was a throwback to a different era. He reminded me very much of 1970s hero Rab Prentice, who could resemble a world-beater one game and then a pub team player the next. But, like Prentice, the fans loved him! At the other end of the team, Craig Levein signed a youngster from Arbroath for £70,000, like Levein himself two decades earlier, 'one for the future'. But Andy Webster would not take long to make a huge impression both at club and international level.

Season 2001/2002 began with an unique occasion – Hearts first ever league game at Almondvale Stadium, home to Livingston FC aka Meadowbank Thistle as was. Livvy's rise through the leagues was fairytale stuff and they also had a Hearts legend coaching them – John Robertson. Livvy beat Hearts 2-1 in that opening game and, yet again, we feared the worst. When do we never? Colin Cameron scored Hearts goal and he also scored the winner against Aberdeen at Tynecastle the following week and two goals against Dundee a fortnight later. But, not for the first time and certainly not the last, Hearts sold their best player just weeks into the new season. The board accepted an offer of £1.75m for Cameron from

Wolverhampton Wanderers and the midfield dynamo was on his way south but not before taking a pot shot at the number of players that had left Tynecastle. Few of the cup winning team now remained. The fans, yet again, were outraged and there were vociferous protests once more against Chris Robinson and the board of directors. Hearts had been stung two years earlier when the talented Paul Ritchie left Tynecastle for nothing – the club had turned down an offer of £1m from Rangers the year before. Clearly, they didn't want their fingers burnt again so the offer for Cameron was gratefully accepted.

Hearts drew with Rangers at Tynecastle shortly after Cameron's departure with another of the seemingly endless supply of young talent at the club – Stephen Simmons – scoring Hearts equaliser. But then a rut followed. Three games without a goal included being knocked out of the League Cup by First Division Ross County on penalty kicks and the doom and gloom had returned. Hearts lost at Easter Road then Pittodrie before Livingston won 3-1 at Tynecastle and the protests resumed with some fury. By now Riccardo Fuller had joined and while he looked dreadfully short of match fitness on his debut at Easter Road, the Jamaican soon came on to a game. He scored in a 3-1 win against Dundee and he seemed to inspire his team mates. Just before Christmas, Fuller scored one of the best goals I've ever seen at Tynecastle when he ran nearly the full length of the pitch before rounding the keeper to seal a 3-1 win against Motherwell. It was awesome and the whole of Tynecastle stood to give their new star a standing ovation.

Hearts won six out of their next seven games, including a Scottish Cup win over Ross County at

Tynecastle and it seemed there was light at the end of the tunnel. There was – an oncoming train in the form of Inverness Caledonian Thistle. Caley had their own inspiration in Dennis Wyness and they breezed to a 3-1 Scottish Cup win at Tynecastle – Hearts first defeat at home in the Scottish Cup for twenty years. The last team to win in Gorgie on Scottish Cup business? Forfar Athletic. Now don't get me started on that...

That took the wind right out of Hearts sails and the fans were despondent once more. Not even the delights of Riccardo Fuller could raise the spirits and the big striker's goals began to dry up amid the realisation his loan period was nearing its end and he would soon be on his way. There was only one other performance of note and that came at Pittodrie where Hearts trailed Aberdeen 2-1 with three minutes to go- but won 3-2 thanks to a great strike from Frenchman Stephane Mahe and a header from Kevin McKenna. It lifted the gloom temporarily.

With Fuller on his way the exit door also opened for Austrian Thomas Flogel, Frenchman Stephane Adam and cup winning captain Stevie Fulton. The trio bode a tearful farewell after Hearts final game of the season – a home defeat by Livingston. Flogel, in particular, did not want to leave a club he came to love and a city he came to love but Hearts could not afford to pay him and Big Tam could not afford such a drop in his pay. Flogel headed back to Austria where he won the league championship with Austria Vienna – and amused the fans afterwards by wearing a Hearts kilt during the celebrations. Once a Jambo, always a Jambo!

It was fair to say Hearts fans weren't exactly looking forward to season 2002/2003. A plethora of players had left the club. With the departure of Flogel, Fulton and Adam, the last of the 1998 cup winning side had gone. That glorious May Day at Celtic Park was now officially confined to the history books. A potential star of the future – Riccardo Fuller – had also gone to the delights of Preston North End. I thought – as most other Hearts fans did – that Craig Levein would be forced to play a bunch of untried and unready kids for season 2002/03. But the story of this great club was about to take another turn.

10

The Future

Bonjour, Bonjour... Hearts fans
celebrate a famous win in Bordeaux,
UEFA Cup November 2003

JULY 2002. Brockville Park, Falkirk. Hearts are playing a pre-season friendly against a team given a reprieve from relegation to the Second Division thanks to the demise of Clydebank. Plenty of players have left Tynecastle during the close season. Only one has arrived – Dutch striker Mark De Vries. And he's injured. There are a couple of trialists one of whom – Frenchman Jean-Louis Valois – looks useful. The rest of the Hearts squad consists of untried youngsters. Hearts huff and puff and require a penalty save from Antti Niemi to secure a 2-2 draw. My fears for the season ahead are far from alleviated. The league season starts at Hearts nemesis – Dens Park. However, it's a better performance from Craig Levein's men as they take an early lead through Gary Wales but have to settle for a 1-1 draw. But I'm satisfied with that and look forward to the visit of Hibernian to Tynecastle the following week.....

My irritation with television dictating dates and kick-off times for games is well documented throughout this book. In 2002, there was much angst in the board-rooms of the Premier League clubs as the much vaunted new deal with SKY Television collapsed. Quite frankly the Scottish game just isn't worth the vast millions the clubs wanted – believed to be nearly £50 million – and the satellite television company walked away. Well, Rupert Murdoch's business covers so many major sporting events these days, the absence of Scottish football wasn't exactly a body blow to them. The lack of a deal, however, was a body blow to Scotland's elite clubs, many of whom had budgeted for a million pounds or so extra income. Motherwell had already sunk into administration and had to make nineteen players redundant so there were fevered brows in boardrooms across the country. It was the B.B.C. who stepped in with a much less lucrative deal but it meant some income – and more matches moved to a Sunday afternoon. The first Edinburgh derby of the season was the first of those games and more than 15,000 fans turned up at Tynecastle on a wet and miserable August Sunday afternoon. From a Hearts fan's viewpoint, the good old Beeb couldn't have picked a better game. It turned out to be one of the most remarkable derbies in over a century of the fixture. Hearts exorcised the ghost of the infamous 6-2 drubbing at Easter Road two years before by hammering the hapless Hibees 5-1 – and striker Mark De Vries, on his home debut, scored four of them – a record for a player playing his inaugural Edinburgh derby. Jean-Louis Valois produced a scintillating performance that tore the Hibs defence to ribbons and De Vries picked up the pieces. Steven Boyack, a player heavily criticised by the Hearts support the previous season, was sublime in midfield while Steven Pressley and Kevin McKenna were immense in defence. Hearts were just 3-1 ahead as injury time approached when De Vries scored two more. When the fifth goal went in I thought the Wheatfield Stand was going to collapse – Tynecastle bounced! The scenes at the end of the game were incredible – it was as if Hearts had won a trophy. We had waited years for a result like that and the bragging rights were back in Gorgie big time. As Scott Wilson, the Tynecastle DJ played Zip-De-Di-Do-

Dah at the end, we bellowed to those Hibs fans who were left '5-1; we only won 5-1!' It was, as Lou Reed sang so memorably, a perfect day.

Hearts start to the league season exceeded all expectations. Just one defeat in the opening eleven games – inevitably to Rangers at Ibrox. The best time then for Hearts to open their annual sale. Goalkeeper Antti Niemi, darling of the fans and Tynecastle legend despite the relatively short time he spent in Gorgie, was on his way to the English Premiership and Southampton. The fee was £2 million, a fee Hearts just could not turn down and with the Finnish star holding ambitions to play at the very highest level there was little Hearts could realistically do to hold him back. Niemi was happy in Edinburgh and spoke highly of the club and Craig Levein. He remains the finest goalkeeper I've seen in a Hearts jersey and, given I've seen the likes of Jim Cruickshank, Henry Smith and Gilles Rousset, I can pay Antti no higher accolade.

We expected Craig Levein to move swiftly to sign the services of another goalkeeper and the Head Coach did make an addition to the squad – a midfield player. Middlesbrough's Phil Stamp was frustrated at not getting a regular place at the Riverside Stadium and moved on a free transfer to Tynecastle. It didn't take Stampy long to make an impression. After scoring a sublime goal at Livingston, the Englishman was to earn cult status in the next derby at Easter Road. Hearts were never going to repeat the 5-1 scoreline but it seemed the expectation of producing the same entertainment levels of that game weighed heavily on the shoulders of those in maroon. It was a desperately poor game and when Hibs went a goal ahead just before half-time things looked bleak for the

JTs. The second half was woeful but there were no more goals and our little Hibby friends were becoming more excited as the game headed towards the final few minutes. In contrast to the game in August Hearts just didn't look like scoring. Craig Levein threw on youngster Neil Janczk in a desperate bid to salvage a draw. The Hibs fans taunted the Dalkeith lad with chants of 'Who the **** are you?' With five minutes left Janczk swung in a deep cross to the head of Kevin McKenna who headed the ball past a static Nick Colgan in the Hibs goal. 1-1 – salvation! Hearts fans jumped for joy – we had denied the Hibees again. With a minute left, Hibs pushed forward, frustrated to only draw a game they seemed to have had in the bag. From defence, Hearts broke up field. The previously unheralded Janczk delivered the perfect pass to Phil Stamp who strode into the penalty box and drove the ball past Colgan. 2-1 to Hearts – jubilation in the Hearts end! Dejected Hibees could scarcely believe it. Hearts had played perhaps their poorest game of the season but still managed to beat the wee team on their own patch. It gave me almost as much satisfaction as the 5-1 game. The surge of adrenalin when Stampy hit the winner was incredible. The Englishman showed he felt the same way by jumping into the stand to celebrate with delirious Jambos – and was promptly booked by fussy referee Willie Young. And as he had been booked already, Stamp was sent off. It mattered not – Hearts had beaten their rivals again!

There was no question of Hearts – or any other team for that matter – mounting any kind of challenge to the Old Firm as Celtic and Rangers were so far ahead of the rest. Well, when you buy your rivals best players – Livingston's Davide Fernandez moved to Celtic Park for

£1 million – you can't expect any serious competition. In the space of four days in December Hearts lost ten goals in two games. A 4-0 tanking at Tynecastle by Rangers was bad enough. Then, injuries and suspensions denied Craig Levein of several players for the trip to face bottom club Motherwell at Fir Park. Alan Maybury, Steven Pressley, Phil Stamp, Scott Severin, Neil Macfarlane and Steven Boyack were all missing and Levein was forced to pitch some untried youngsters into the first team. It didn't work. Hearts lost 6-1 to a Motherwell team inspired by James McFadden. From the sublime to the ridiculous.

Hearts recovered to put in a steady league challenge and they gave Celtic a fright at Celtic Park on Boxing Day when, despite taking an early lead, Hearts lost 4-2. Celtic manager Martin O'Neill praised Hearts to the hilt afterwards stating it was a magnificent game of football with Hearts making a real game of it. A few days later it was time for our friends across the city to visit Tynecastle for the New Year Derby, played on January 2nd 2003. And another day of emotional turmoil for fans of the team in green and white.

Hearts didn't have the best of days defensively. Hibs raced into an early two goal lead and I sat with my head in my hands for most of the first half. My mood wasn't helped by the sight of Hibs player Ian Murray having '7-0' shaved on the back of his head, an obvious reference to the thirtieth anniversary of a certain derby game in the 1970s. Steven Pressley pulled a goal back with a penalty just before half-time and with twenty minutes to go, the new Hammer of the Hibs – Mark De Vries – scored a fine equaliser. Hearts had come back from the dead! As the game headed for a 2-2 draw, Hibs scored twice in the last five minutes to go 4-2 in front. The fourth goal followed a missed penalty kick but Gary O'Connor followed up the rebound following Roddy McKenzie's save. At that point, I headed for the exits. The Hibs fans in the Roseburn Stand were beside themselves with joy. It looked like sweet revenge for them. As I headed towards the stairs heading out of Tynecastle, a muted cheer was raised by the home support. Substitute Graham Weir had nodded home a third goal for Hearts. Scant consolation I thought as I headed for the Station Tavern. Seconds later, bedlam. Hearts had raced up the park once more – and Weir stroked a glorious shot past Colgan. 4-4! Four bloody four!! It was the great escape – and more! The game ended with honours even – but for Hearts such a miraculous escape felt like a victory. Once again Hearts had denied Hibs a win. Happy New Weir!

That was the last game before the winter break. No games for three weeks. Hearts took their players to the sun of Portugal for a week and, in retrospect, perhaps it was the worst thing they could have done. They returned to a bitter January afternoon at Brockville Park for a Scottish Cup tie with First Division leaders Falkirk. I stood on the crumbling terrace with a restricted view with a bitter wind blowing in rain and sleet. With half an hour gone, Craig Levein brought on Andy Webster. Well it was a token gesture by the Head Coach. Hearts were already four goals down. The 4,000 strong travelling support could scarcely believe it. It was the Fir Park debacle all over again. Except this was Hearts supposedly strongest team with the exception of young goalkeeper Craig Gordon who had replaced injury victim Roddy McKenzie. But Gordon could not be blamed for any of the four goals. There was no further scoring and

Hearts were out of the Scottish Cup at the first embarrassing round. It was almost ten years to the day that Hearts had lost 6-0 at the very same ground. I stormed out of Brockville in 1993 vowing never to watch Hearts again. I was perilously close to making the same fruitless vow a decade later.

The Falkirk game seemed to be another bitter lesson for what was essentially a young Hearts team. The players buckled down and finished the league campaign strongly. They easily achieved a top six finish – the Premier League remained fixated by this ludicrous split after thirty three games which saw the top six play each other once more and the bottom six do likewise – thereby becoming the only team outside of the Old Firm to achieve a top six finish in each of the seasons since it had been introduced. Unfortunately, the lesser team in Edinburgh had a penchant for losing late goals and finished seventh – so the opportunity for humiliating Hibs for a fourth time that season was gone. Despite a limited squad and having to play youngsters and players out of position, Hearts finished in third place in the Premier League. The best of the rest as they say. And in doing so qualified for the U.E.F.A. Cup for season 2003/2004. Craig Levein had done an astounding job and there was a growing sign of maturity and self-belief when Hearts defeated Celtic at Tynecastle in April thanks to a screamer of a last minute goal from Austin McCann. It was Hearts first victory over either of the Old Firm for three years and effectively killed Celtic's championship challenge. A significant victory.

Season 2002/2003 had more ups and downs than a liftman's nightmare but at the end of the season Hearts finished third in the Premier League, qualified for

Europe, reached the semi-finals of the League Cup and gained two memorable Edinburgh derby victories over Hibernian. Add on a tumultuous recovery in the New Year derby and a long awaited victory over Celtic then it was, all things considered, a season to remember. In my view the Scottish Cup defeat at Falkirk was particularly hard to take as, given the way the subsequent draws worked out and Celtic losing to Inverness Caledonian Thistle for the second time in three years, Hearts would have been a fair bet to get all the way to the final. And, as in 1998, a leaden footed Rangers may have been there for the taking. But I shouldn't dwell on what might have been.

At the time of writing the future for Hearts is uncertain. There is the very real possibility of Hearts moving away from Tynecastle to Murrayfield, the home of Scottish rugby. Chief Executive Chris Robinson says Tynecastle is no longer fit for purpose with the pitch too small to meet U.E.F.A. rules and a main stand that is crumbling and giving serious safety concerns. With the club already nearly £18m in debt, the sale of Tynecastle will greatly reduce this financial burden (although not, I suspect, completely clear it) The idea of Hearts moving along the road caused a mixed reaction initially, but early in 2004, those vehemently opposed to moving are growing in numbers. Traditionalists are appalled. The Heart of Midlothian Supporters Trust has called on Robinson to resign. Personally, the idea of moving away from Gorgie dismays me but it seems the argument that Tynecastle is no longer fit for purpose is a strong one. I'd watch Hearts if they decided to play halfway up Arthur's Seat (although this would only further encourage the long ball game....) and if the move to Murrayfield saves the club then so be it. But I won't be the only one in tears if it happens. So if there are any billionaires out there, what we need is someone to clear Hearts debt and rebuild the main stand – that way only European fixtures need to be played at Murrayfield....

As I type this final chapter, we're midway through season 2003/2004. Hearts began the season with new signings Dennis Wyness, Paul Hartley and Patrick Kisnorbo. But we still managed to lose to ten man Hibs at Easter Road....... However, a glamour U.E.F.A. Cup tie with French aces Bordeaux was one of the highlights of the campaign. I joined 3,500 other Jambos in the south of France on a magical day when the Scots won the hearts of their French hosts and a memorable day was had by all – made more memorable by the fact that Mark de Vries scored a late winner to give Hearts an unlikely but famous 1-0 win. Typically, the maroons undid that magnificent effort by losing the return leg at Tynecastle 2-0, so going out of the competition on a 2-1 aggregate. A small consolation was the fact that the city of Bordeaux made a presentation to the Hearts support in recognition of their behaviour in the south of France – a proud moment for all those in maroon and white who made the epic journey.

It's by chance that I'm a Hearts supporter in the first place. Had my father not wanted to try and shelter me from the bigotry of the Old Firm in the 1960s, I may well have been a Blue Nose or a Tim. Had Falkirk played anyone else on that fateful day in 1968, I would almost certainly still be a Bairn and would have found that Scottish Cup result in January 2003 as one of the best displays ever by a Falkirk team (damn them!) But fate decreed I would be a Jambo. Follow the Hearts and you can't go wrong says the club's anthem. A misplaced sentiment if ever there was one! Hearts have shaped my life for more than thirty-five years and will continue to do so for as long as there is a Heart of Midlothian Football Club and I'm still on this earth.

To the thousands of other Jambos who feel the same way – this book is for you.

INDEX

Lightning Source UK Ltd.
Milton Keynes UK
25 November 2010

163442UK00001B/58/A

9 781904 623076